DISCERNING THE PLIGHT OF
MAN

PAUL DAVID WASHER

"Paul Washer possesses a rare gift that combines theological precision with penetrating application that is heart-searching and life-changing. This workbook will lead you to a better understanding of critically important issues that form the foundation of your knowledge of who God is and how we are to relate to Him. Washer does an exceptional job of magnifying the sovereignty of God, while exposing the deplorable depths of our sin. In so doing, this book wonderfully magnifies the saving, sanctifying grace of God in ways that will first humble your soul and then cause your heart to soar to the heights of the throne of grace. Read this workbook carefully, answer its questions thoughtfully, and you will find your spiritual life enhanced greatly."

— Dr. Steven J. Lawson, President and Founder of OnePassion Ministries

"What we have here is a no-holds-barred, deeply biblical workbook on the doctrine of the human race. It has everything, and I mean everything—from the fall, through our moral inability to seek God, His hatred of both sin and sinner, and the reality and terror of hell…. I kid you not, we will be using this manual to train our people at Niddrie Community Church (and further afield). Hard, hard truths are here made understandable and without pulling punches."

— Mez McConnell, Director of 20schemes, Author of *Is There Anybody Out There?*

"Paul Washer greatly encourages me, because he refuses to neglect why the church exists—that we are here to be a tabernacle of witness in the wilderness of this world. May God use this book to remind us that hell is a reality and that we have a responsibility to warn every man, that we may present every man perfect in Jesus Christ."

— Ray Comfort, Founder and CEO of Living Waters

DISCERNING THE PLIGHT OF **MAN**

Copyright 2023 Paul David Washer

Published by:

HeartCry Missionary Society
PO Box 7372
Roanoke, VA 24019

www.heartcrymissionary.com

Printed in the United States of America 2023
ESV Edition 2A, Second Printing

Unless otherwise noted, all Scripture quotations taken from the
The Holy Bible, English Standard Version® (ESV®)
Copyright 2001 by Crossway, a publishing ministry of Good News Publishers.
All rights reserved. ESV Text Edition: 2016.
Note: Pronouns referring to God have been capitalized for consistency.

Edited by Forrest Hite and Elzeline Hite
Additional proofreading by Hunter Gately
Layout and design by Jon Green, Matthew Robinson, Forrest Hite, and Michael Reece

DISCERNING THE PLIGHT OF MAN

Table of Contents

Introduction

METHOD OF STUDY

The great goal of this study is for the student to have an encounter with God through His Word. Founded upon the conviction that the Scriptures are the inspired and infallible Word of God, this study has been designed in such a way that it is literally impossible for the student to advance without an open Bible before him or her. The goal is to help the reader obey the exhortation of the Apostle Paul in II Timothy 2:15:

> *Do your best to present yourself to God as one approved, a worker*
> *who has no need to be ashamed, rightly handling the word of truth.*

Each chapter deals with a specific aspect of the doctrine of man and his desperate plight before a holy God. The student will complete each chapter by answering the questions and following the instructions according to the Scriptures given. The student is encouraged to meditate upon each text and write his or her thoughts. The benefit gained from this study will depend upon the student's investment. If the student answers the questions thoughtlessly, merely copying the text without seeking to understand its meaning, this book will be of very little help.

Discerning the Plight of Man is primarily a biblical study and does not contain much in the way of colorful illustrations, quaint stories, or theological treatises. It was the desire of the author to provide a work that simply points the way to the Scriptures and allows the Word of God to speak for itself.

This workbook may be used by an individual, in a small group, for a Sunday school class, or in other contexts. It is highly recommended that the student complete each chapter on his or her own before meeting for discussion and questions with a group or discipleship leader.

EXHORTATION TO THE STUDENT

The student is encouraged to study biblical doctrine and discover its exalted place in the Christian life. The true Christian cannot bear or even survive a divorce between the emotions and the intellect or between devotion to God and the doctrine of God. According to the Scriptures, neither our emotions nor our experiences provide an adequate foundation for the Christian life. Only the truths of Scripture, understood with the mind and communicated through doctrine, can provide that sure foundation upon which we should establish our beliefs and our behavior and determine the validity of our emotions and experiences. The mind is not the enemy of the heart, and doctrine is not an obstacle to devotion. The two are indispensable and should be inseparable. The Scriptures command us to love the Lord our God with all our heart, with all our soul, and with all our mind (Matthew 22:37) and to worship God both in spirit and in truth (John 4:24).

The study of doctrine is both an intellectual and devotional discipline. It is a passionate search for God that should always lead the student to greater personal transformation, obedience, and heartfelt worship. Therefore, the student should be on guard against the great error of seeking only impersonal knowledge instead of the person of God. Neither mindless devotion nor mere intellectual pursuits are profitable, for in either case, God is lost.

THE ENGLISH STANDARD VERSION

The English Standard Version is required to complete this study. This is an accurate translation that has become the Bible of choice for millions of Christians around the globe. This workbook is also available for use with the New American Standard Bible (heartcrymissionary.com/books).

A WORD FROM THE AUTHOR

Apart from a correct understanding of the nature and sin of man, it is impossible to understand the gospel of Jesus Christ or to appreciate fully the grace that God has extended to us through this magnificent work. For this reason, this workbook purposes to set before the reader the reality of man's fallenness and the dire consequences of his sin. The purpose is not to steal hope from the heart of the reader, but to point the reader to the only true hope for man—the gospel of Jesus Christ. In other words, this workbook takes the reader through the dark tunnel of man's sin so that he or she might see with greater clarity the light of God's grace.

I would like to thank my wife Charo for her timely encouragement in every endeavor and my four children (Ian, Evan, Rowan, and Bronwyn), who continue to be a great blessing. I would also like to thank HeartCry staff member Forrest Hite for his diligent and meticulous editing of the several different manuscripts that he has received. His contributions to the arrangement and overall readability of this work are as significant as they are appreciated. My thanks are also extended to the entire staff at HeartCry, who have been a great encouragement throughout the process of this book's writing and publication.

A WORD FROM THE EDITOR

Discerning the Plight of Man is derived from Paul Washer's previously published work, *The Truth About Man*; it has been expanded, revised, and modified. Due to the close relationship between the two books, those who have studied *The Truth About Man* will likely recognize a fair amount of the material in this workbook. Compared to its predecessor, this work contains (1) more than one hundred and twenty brand-new notes; (2) several new points and sub-points; (3) numerous other changes and alterations to both the content and the layout; and (4) improved flow and readability due to a multi-step editing process. It is my belief that *Discerning the Plight of Man* will prove beneficial to all, regardless of familiarity with *The Truth About Man*.

RECOMMENDED RESOURCES FOR FURTHER STUDIES

Created in God's Image by Anthony Hoekema
The Christian View of Man by J. Gresham Machen
Not the Way It's Supposed to Be by Cornelius Plantinga, Jr.
The Imputation of Adam's Sin by John Murray
On the Bondage of the Will by Martin Luther
The Sinfulness of Sin by Ralph Venning
Human Nature in Its Fourfold State by Thomas Boston (for advanced students)
Gleanings from the Scriptures: Man's Total Depravity by Arthur W. Pink (for advanced students)

ADDITIONAL NOTE

You may have noticed that this book is being sold at a strange price. Here's why: one dollar ($) from every copy sold will go directly to fund mission work through HeartCry Missionary Society (heartcrymissionary.com). The rest of the sale price is just enough to cover the cost of printing, publication, and distribution. The author is not profiting from the sale of this book, nor has he profited from the sale of any other book. Over the years, we have utilized and explored many avenues in order to publish these workbooks. Ultimately, we have reached the conclusion that doing so in-house at a low cost, even with slightly lower quality, is the most effective way of getting these useful tools into the hands of as many people across the globe as possible. We hope and pray that the Lord continues to use these books to point His people to His Word unto the edification of His church.

Optional Study Schedule

Week One: The Creation and Fall of Man

Day 1: Preface
       Chapter 1, Main Points 1-2
Day 2: Chapter 1, Main Points 3-5
Day 3: Chapter 2
Day 4: Chapter 3
Day 5: Chapter 4

Week Two: The Truth About Man, Part 1

Day 1: Chapter 5, Section 1
       Chapter 5, Section 2, Main Points 1-2
Day 2: Chapter 5, Section 2, Main Points 3-5
Day 3: Chapter 6, Main Points 1-2
Day 4: Chapter 6, Main Points 3-4
Day 5: Chapter 7

Week Three: The Truth About Man, Part 2

Day 1: Chapter 8
Day 2: Chapter 9
Day 3: Chapter 10
Day 4: Chapter 11, Section 1
       Chapter 11, Section 2, Main Point 1
Day 5: Chapter 11, Section 2, Main Points 2-4

Week Four: God's Disposition Toward the Sinner

Day 1: Chapter 12
Day 2: Chapter 13
Day 3: Chapter 14
Day 4: Chapter 15
Day 5: Chapter 16

Week Five: God's Judgments in the Sinner's Life

Day 1: Chapter 17, Section 1
       Chapter 17, Section 2, Main Points 1-2
Day 2: Chapter 17, Section 2, Main Points 3-7
Day 3: Chapter 18
Day 4: Chapter 19, Main Points 1-2
Day 5: Chapter 19, Main Points 3-5

Week Six: God's Judgment of Death

Day 1:   Chapter 20
         Chapter 21, Section 1, Main Points 1-2
Day 2:   Chapter 21, Section 1, Main Points 3-4
Day 3:   Chapter 21, Section 2
Day 4:   Chapter 22, Section 1
         Chapter 22, Section 2, Main Point 1
Day 5:   Chapter 22, Section 2, Main Points 2-5

Week Seven: Final Judgment, Hell, and the Hope of the Gospel

Day 1:   Chapter 23, Main Points 1-4
Day 2:   Chapter 23, Main Points 5-6
Day 3:   Chapter 24, Sections 1-3
Day 4:   Chapter 24, Section 4
         Chapter 25
Day 5:   Chapter 26

DISCERNING THE PLIGHT OF MAN

Preface: Explanation of Purpose

Before the student begins working through this manual, he or she must understand something of its content and purpose. In this study, we will consider man's sin and the response of a holy God against him. We will attempt to sound the depths of man's moral depravity and the acts of sin that result from what man has become. We will also consider God's response to man in his fallen state and continual rebellion. Finally, we will focus primarily upon man's hostility to God and God's judgment of the sinner with little reference to God's love or his redemptive work in Christ. The reason for this unusual omission is fourfold: (1) that the student might understand the horrid moral condition of man apart from the grace of God; (2) that the student might understand the terrible predicament of man before the justice and wrath of God; (3) that the student might understand the extent to which God's justice had to be satisfied in order to appease His wrath; and (4) that the student might better appreciate the grace of God toward the sinner that has been revealed through the gospel of Jesus Christ.

For the reasons mentioned above, working through this manual will not be easy. Each turn of the page will lead us down a narrow tunnel that will grow darker with every step until we find ourselves drawing near to hell itself. We will see man as we perhaps have never seen him before, and we will see certain aspects of God that are often avoided and too infrequently proclaimed with clarity. This manual is a forced march through the open wound of man's moral corruption. It is a summons to behold God in all His fury against sin and the sinner. It is a necessary darkness through which we must wander in order that we might appreciate the light when it comes. Only by beholding man in his utter sinfulness and beholding God in His perfect righteousness and judgment can we truly appreciate the love of God that sent us a Savior!

> We shall never have an adequate conception of the greatness of this salvation unless we realize something at any rate of what we were before this mighty power took hold of us, unless we realize what we would still be if God had not intervened in our lives and had rescued us. In other words, we must realize the depth of sin, what sin really means, and what it has done to the human race.[1]

> Without a knowledge of our unfaithfulness and rebellion we will never come to know God as the God of truth and grace. Without a knowledge of our pride we will never know Him in His greatness. Nor will we come to Him for the healing we need. When we are sick physically and know that we are sick, we seek out a doctor and follow his prescription for a cure. But if we did not know we were sick, we would not seek help and might well perish from the illness. It is the same spiritually. If we think we are well, we will never accept God's cure; we think we do not need it. Instead, if by God's grace we become aware of our sickness—actually, of something worse than sickness, of spiritual death so far as any meaningful response to God is concerned—then we have a basis for understanding the meaning of Christ's work on our behalf, and can embrace Him as Savior and be transformed by Him.[2]

[1] Dr. Martyn Lloyd-Jones, *Ephesians*, Vol.2, p.14
[2] James Montgomery Boyce, *Foundations of the Christian Faith*, p.198

There is no better way of testing our understanding of the Christian doctrine of salvation than to examine our understanding of the true nature of sin.[3]

Finally, it is strongly recommended that students in some way pair this workbook with the preceding one, *Discovering the Glorious Gospel*. As mentioned above, *Discerning the Plight of Man* contains many hard truths and few comforting ones. In this book, the student will hopefully be brought to realize the truly desperate nature of his plight—because of his own wickedness and moral corruption and because of God's righteousness and judgment. In *Discovering the Glorious Gospel*, however, the student learns that the God of justice and wrath is also a God of love, who has done the incomprehensible by sending His Son to reconcile fallen man and transform him into a child of God. It could therefore lead one to despair excessively if he or she were only to focus on the biblical truths laid out in this manual without seriously considering the glorious hope of the gospel.

---

[3] Dr. Martyn Lloyd-Jones, *Romans*, Vol.6, p.119

PART ONE

THE CREATION AND FALL OF MAN

Chapter 1: The Creation of Man

The Scriptures teach us that man is neither an accident nor the result of some mindless process; rather, man is the creative work of the eternal God. After God had created all other creatures, He formed the first man, Adam, from the dust of the ground. God then breathed the breath of life into Adam's nostrils, and he became a living being. From Adam, God formed the woman Eve to be both his companion and his helper. They were commanded to multiply and fill the earth, which had been placed under their dominion. All mankind finds its common ancestry in this union of Adam and Eve.

The Scripture is clear that both man and woman were created **by** God and **for** God and find meaning for their existence only in loving Him, glorifying Him, and doing His will. Unique among all other creatures, they alone were created in the **imago dei**—the image of God—and granted the privilege of living in personal and unbroken fellowship with Him.

These truths are of great importance for us because they define who we are and the purpose for which we were made. We are not the authors of our own existence; we were brought into existence by the gracious will and power of God. We do not belong to ourselves, but to God who made us for His own purposes and good pleasure. To seek to separate from God is to attempt to sever ourselves from life itself. To live independently of His person and will is to deny the purpose for which we were made.

1. In the second chapter of Genesis is found Scripture's account of the creation of man. Summarize this account as described in Genesis 2:7. What does this passage communicate to us about the origin of man and about his relationship to God?

_____

_____

_____

_____

_____

_____

NOTES: In this text, both the glory and the humility of man are revealed. The glory of man is revealed in that his creation was the result of a special and personal act of God. The humility of man is revealed in that he was created from the dust of the earth; therefore, his existence and glory are totally dependent upon God. Apart from God, man is little more than lifeless dust.

2. Also in the second chapter of Genesis is found Scripture's account of the creation of the first woman, Eve. Summarize this account as described in Genesis 2:21-23. What does this passage communicate to us about woman's origin and about her relationship to both God and man?

_____

_____

_____

_____

_____

_____

NOTES: Unlike man, who was created out of the dust of the ground, the woman was created from the man. This fact communicates several important truths, the most prominent of which are: (1) like man, woman was created as a special, personal work of God and is therefore man's equal before God; and (2) although the woman was given a different role from man's (Genesis 2:20), both are interdependent. The Apostle Paul writes in I Corinthians 11:11-12: "Nevertheless, in the Lord woman is not independent of man nor man of woman; for as woman was made from man, so man is now born of woman. And all things are from God."

3. Having established the truth that man is the creative work of God, we must now consider his uniqueness among the rest of creation. According to the following phrases from Genesis 1:26, how is man unique compared to the rest of creation?

   a. *Let Us make man.*

_____

_____

_____

_____

_____

NOTES: God did not say, "Let there be," as with the rest of creation (vv.3, 6, 14); instead He said, "Let Us make." This communicates the idea of a greater personal relationship. The plural forms in the phrases "Let Us" and "Our image" have led to a great deal of speculation. Since neither the text nor the context reveal the answer, we should proceed with caution. We may, however, make the following statements. **First**, it is probably not a reference to angels or some angelic court, since the act of creation is always attributed exclusively to God. **Second**, it may reveal the mind of God and reinforce the truth that creation is the result of God's decree alone. **Third**, it may be Scripture's first revelation of the plurality of persons within the Trinity—Father, Son, and Holy Spirit. This would certainly not contradict the rest of Scripture, which sees creation as a work of the Father, the Son (John 1:1-3; Colossians 1:16), and the Spirit (Genesis 1:2).

b. *In Our image.*

_____

_____

_____

_____

_____

NOTES: God did not say, "according to its kind," as with the rest of creation (vv.11-12, 21, 24-25); instead He said, "in Our image." Humanity is unique among creation in that it alone is said to bear the **imago dei** or "image of God." The "image of God" may refer to several ideas. **Personality** – Adam and Eve were personal and self-conscious creatures. They were not mere animals driven by instinct or machines programmed to respond to certain stimuli. **Spirituality** – The Scriptures declare that "God is spirit" (John 4:24), and so it is reasonable to expect to find this same attribute in man, since he was created in God's image. Adam and Eve were more than animated clay. They were spiritual, endowed with a genuine capacity to know God; fellowship with God; and respond to God in obedience, adoration, and thanksgiving. **Knowledge** – In Colossians 3:10, the Scriptures describe one aspect of being in the image of God as "being renewed in knowledge" of God. This does not mean that Adam and Eve knew all that can be known about God—a finite creature can never fully comprehend an infinite God. Rather, it means that the knowledge they did possess was pure or unalloyed. **Self-Determination or Will** – Adam and Eve were created with a will. They possessed the power of self-determination, and they were granted the freedom to choose. **Immortality** – Although Adam and Eve were created (and therefore had a beginning) and although every moment of their very existence depended upon the kindness of their Creator, they were endowed with an immortal soul—once created, it would never cease to exist. The immortality of the soul should lead all men to consider carefully the awesome responsibility of self-determination. Since the soul is eternal, the choices we make will bear eternal consequences from which there is no escape.

c. *Let them have dominion.*

_____

_____

_____

_____

> **NOTES:** Man and woman were given the privilege and responsibility of ruling over all creation as vice-regents of God. Their rule was not to be independent of God's rule, but in perfect conformity to His will. They were to rule for the benefit and care of creation and for the glory of God.

4. In Genesis 1:26, we learned that man is unique among the rest of creation in that he alone was created in the image of God. In the following Scriptures, we will discover that, although man is unique, he shares a common purpose with the rest of creation—he was not made for himself, but for the glory and good pleasure of God. What do the following Scriptures teach us about creation's primary purpose?

a. *Psalm 104:31-35*

_____

_____

_____

_____

_____

> **NOTES:** The great goal of man is not to strive independently of God for the attainment of his own personal happiness. Man was created for God's good pleasure or gladness. The great goal of man is to seek God's good pleasure and in that to find the meaning of his own existence and the fullness of delight.

b. *Romans 11:36*

_____

_____

_____

_____

_____

_____

NOTES: Here the Apostle Paul draws a perfect circle. Man's life originates with God; it continues through God; and it reaches its ultimate goal in bringing glory, honor, and praise to God.

c. *Colossians 1:16*

_____

_____

_____

_____

_____

_____

NOTES: It is important to understand that this verse refers specifically to the Son of God. It was the Father's good pleasure to create the world through His Son and for His Son. In this small preposition "for" we find the meaning of our very existence. Man, together with the rest of creation, was made for God, His glory, and His good pleasure.

5. The Scriptures teach that man and woman were created **by** God and **for** God; and they find meaning for their existence only in loving Him, glorifying Him, and doing His will. We are not the authors of our own existence; we were brought into existence by the gracious will and power of God. We do not belong to ourselves, but to God, who made us for His own purposes

and good pleasure. In light of these great truths, how should mankind respond? Write your thoughts on the proper responses listed below and the Scriptures that elicit them.

a. *Reverence (Psalm 33:6-9)*

b. *Worship (Psalm 95:6)*

c. *Service (Psalm 100:2-4)*

d. *Love (Mark 12:30)*

_____

_____

_____

_____

_____

e. *Glory and Honor (I Corinthians 10:31)*

_____

_____

_____

_____

_____

Chapter 2: The Fall of Adam

In accordance with His own purpose and good pleasure, God created Adam and Eve and commanded them not to eat of the tree of knowledge of good and evil. Obedience to the command would lead to a life of joyful fellowship with God and continued dominion over creation. Disobedience to the command would lead to spiritual and physical death and all the accompanying maladies.

According to the Scriptures, Adam and Eve were tempted and disobeyed the command. Because of their disobedience, their fellowship with God was broken, and they fell from their original state of righteousness and holiness. These devastating consequences of Adam's disobedience were not limited to him alone, but resulted in the fall of the entire human race. Although the Scriptures do not remove all mystery surrounding this great truth, they affirm that the sin and guilt of Adam has been imputed or credited to all his descendants and that all men—without exception—are now born bearing Adam's fallen nature and exhibiting his hostility toward God.

1. In Genesis 2:16-17, we find the commandment and the warning given to Adam. Read the text until you are familiar with its contents, and then answer the following questions.

   a. *According to verse 16, what privilege did God give to Adam? How does this privilege prove that God cared about Adam and did not disregard his needs?*

   _____

   _____

   _____

   _____

   _____

   b. *According to verse 17, what prohibition was placed upon Adam? What was Adam commanded not to do?*

   _____

   _____

   _____

   _____

c. *According to verse 17, what would be penalty for disobeying God's command?*

_____

_____

_____

_____

NOTES: The penalty for Adam's sin would be death. This death would be not only physical but also spiritual. He would become responsive to every sort of wicked stimuli, both human and demonic, and unresponsive to the person and will of God. This truth will be further considered in Chapters 6-9.

2. In Genesis 3:1-6 is found the biblical account of Adam and Eve's temptation to disobey God's command. Read the text until you are familiar with its contents, and then answer the following questions.

a. *In verse 1, the Scriptures declare that a real serpent tempted Eve. According to Revelation 12:9 and 20:2, who was the one working in and through the serpent?*

_____

_____

_____

_____

b. *According to verses 4-5, what promise did Satan make to Eve?*

_____

_____

_____

_____

NOTES: It is helpful to note the craftiness and subtlety with which Satan advanced his argument. First, he distorted God's word to deny God's goodness: "Did God actually say, 'You shall not eat of **any** tree in the garden'?" (v.1; emphasis added). Then, he denied God's word outright: "You will not surely die" (v.4). Finally, he promised Eve that she would be like God, knowing good and evil (v.5).

c. *According to verse 6, how did Eve and her husband Adam respond to Satan's temptation through the serpent?*

_____

_____

_____

_____

NOTES: Their response is a powerful illustration of the following warnings from the Scriptures: (1) "For all that is in the world—the desires of the flesh and the desires of the eyes and the pride of life—is not from the Father but is from the world" (I John 2:16); and (2) "But each person is tempted when he is lured and enticed by his own desire. Then desire when it has conceived gives birth to sin, and sin when it is fully grown brings forth death" (James 1:14-15).

3. The immediate results of Adam and Eve's disobedience are recorded in Genesis 3:7-10. Read the text several times until you are familiar with its contents, and then write your thoughts on the following portions. What were the immediate results of their disobedience?

a. *Verse 7*

_____

_____

_____

_____

_____

b. *Verses 8-10*

_____

_____

_____

_____

_____

NOTES: With one act of disobedience, Adam and Eve fell from their original state of righteousness into moral corruption. Their hearts and minds were no longer pure, but became defiled and shameful. The coverings made from fig leaves were a feeble attempt to hide their sin and corruption. Sin always results in fear and separation from God. Sinful man runs from God's holy presence and fears His righteous judgment.

4. Having considered the immediate results of Adam's disobedience, we will now consider the divine judgments that fell upon the serpent, Eve, and Adam. Read Genesis 3:14-24, and then describe these judgments, which have affected us all.

   a. *The Divine Judgment upon the Serpent (vv.14-15)*

_____

_____

_____

_____

_____

NOTES: The divine judgment which falls upon the serpent is one of ongoing humiliation, shame, and contempt. The judgment is not limited to the physical serpent; it also reaches the fallen spiritual being who worked in and through it: Satan.

b. *The Divine Judgment upon the Woman (v.16)*

_____

_____

_____

_____

_____

_____

NOTES: The clause, "your desire shall be contrary to your husband," is literally, "toward your husband will be your desire." It may denote the following: (1) the woman's relationship with her husband would be marked by longing and lack of fulfillment; (2) the woman, who sought independence from God, would now have an inordinate desire or craving for man; and (3) the relationship between man and woman would be marked by conflict. The woman would "desire" to dominate her husband, and her husband would in turn exploit his authority over her.

c. *The Divine Judgment upon the Man (vv.17-19)*

_____

_____

_____

_____

_____

_____

NOTES: The judgment that fell upon the man can be summed up in three words: toil, futility, and death. This has been the plight of man in every generation since. Even the most powerful and wealthiest of men have been unable to escape this judgment. Regardless of their exploits, they have all laid down their head in death and lost all that they had gained.

5. Although the history of Adam and Eve is beyond tragic, it does not end without hope. In Genesis 3:15, in the midst of the divine judgment of the serpent, is found one of the greatest promises of salvation in the entire Bible. Many Bible scholars refer to it as the **protevangelium** [Latin: **proto** = first + **evangelium** = gospel]. Meditate upon the text, and then describe and explain the promise that is found in the midst of judgment.

_____

_____

_____

_____

_____

_____

_____

NOTES: Jesus Christ is the "offspring" or seed of the woman Mary. On the cross, Satan bruised Christ's heel (*i.e.* Christ was wounded, but not mortally—He rose again from the dead). However, through the same cross, Christ bruised Satan on the head (*i.e.* Satan was mortally wounded—he has been forever defeated). See also Matthew 12:29; Mark 1:24; Luke 10:18; John 12:31; 16:11; I Corinthians 15:24; Colossians 2:15; Hebrews 2:14; I John 3:8.

Chapter 3: Important Questions About the Fall

The Scriptural account of the fall of Adam provides the only adequate explanation of man's present fallen state and the evil that surrounds us. It is also upon this dark background that the glories of God's mercy and grace appear. Only to the degree that we understand the tragedy of Adam and his condemnation can we comprehend something of the glories of Christ and His gospel.

In our study of the fall, we are faced with some of the most important and complex theological concepts in all of Scripture—the origin of evil, the nature of human freedom, the sovereignty of God, and His eternal purpose. Although what we know about these issues will always be mingled with a certain degree of mystery, it is necessary that we endeavor to know what we can. In the following, we will address three questions. **First**, how could Adam—a righteous and holy being—fall? **Second**, did God ordain the fall? **Third**, what is God's eternal purpose in the fall?

HOW COULD ADAM FALL?

The Scriptures affirm that the fall was not due to any fault in the Creator. All of God's works are perfect (Deuteronomy 32:4), He cannot be tempted by sin, and He does not tempt others with sin (James 1:13). The blame for the fall rests squarely upon the shoulders of Adam. As Ecclesiastes 7:29 declares, "See, this alone I found, that God made man upright, but they have sought out many schemes."

From this truth comes one of the greatest theological problems in all the Scriptures: how is it possible that a creature created in the image of God came to choose evil and sin? Adam and Eve had a true inclination toward good, and there was nothing corrupt or evil in them to which temptation might appeal. How such righteous beings could choose evil over good and choose the words of a serpent over the commands of their Creator is beyond human comprehension.

There have been numerous attempts throughout history to explain the fall of Adam, but none of them is without its limitations. We must therefore be content with the simple truth of Scripture that, although God made man righteous and holy, he was finite and mutable (*i.e.* subject to change) and capable of making a choice contrary to the will of God.

DID GOD ORDAIN THE FALL?

The word "ordain" means, "to put in order, arrange, or appoint." Thus, to ask if God ordained the fall is to ask if He arranged or appointed it. Other words that carry similar meaning are "decree," "predetermine," and "predestine." Did God decree or determine beforehand that the fall should occur? The answer to this question is "yes," but we must be very careful to understand what this means and what it does not mean.

God's ordaining of the fall **does not mean** that He forced Satan to tempt our first parents or that He coerced Adam and Eve to disregard His command. What God's creatures did, they did willingly. God is holy, just, and good. He is not the author of sin, He does not sin, He cannot be tempted by sin, and He does not tempt anyone to sin.

God's ordaining of the fall **does mean** that it was certain to happen. It was God's will that Adam be tested, and it was God's will to let Adam both stand and fall alone without the divine aid that could have kept him from falling. God could have hindered Satan from laying the temptation before Eve, or He could have given Adam special sustaining grace in the face of such temptation to enable him to triumph over it. However, from the testimony of Scripture, we understand that He did not.

Finally, God's ordaining of the fall also **does mean** that it was a part of His eternal plan. Before the foundation of the world, before the creation of Adam and Eve and the serpent that tempted them, before the existence of any garden or tree, God ordained the fall for His glory and the greater good of His creation. He did not merely permit our first parents to be tempted and then wait to react to whatever choice they made. He did not merely look through the "corridors of time" and see the fall. Rather, the fall was always a part of God's eternal plan, and He predetermined or predestined that it should and would happen. There is a question that immediately arises from such a statement:

Is God the author of sin?

This question can and should be answered with a strong **negative**. God is not the author of sin, nor does He coerce men to sin against Him. Although He predetermined that the fall should and would happen, He also predetermined that it should happen through the willing actions of Satan, Adam, and Eve. Our finite minds cannot fully comprehend how God can be absolutely sovereign over every event of history and over every individual act without eliminating individual freedom; nevertheless, the Scriptures abound with examples that demonstrate this to be true. Joseph was sold into slavery as a result of the willful sin of his brothers, yet when the final story was told, Joseph declared: "As for you, you meant evil against me, **but God meant it for good**, to bring it about that many people should be kept alive, as they are today" (Genesis 50:20; emphasis added). The Son of God was crucified as a result of man's willful sin and hostility toward God, yet God had ordained the death of Christ before the foundation of the world.

> *This Jesus, delivered up according to the definite plan and foreknowledge of God, you crucified and killed by the hands of lawless men. (Acts 2:23)*

> *For truly in this city they were gathered together against Your holy servant Jesus, whom You anointed, both Herod and Pontius Pilate, along with the Gentiles and the peoples of Israel, to do whatever Your hand and Your purpose had predestined to take place. (Acts 4:27-28)*

In the Scriptures, we see that God does ordain events to occur and then brings them to pass through the willful sin of men—without being the author of their sin or coercing them to do that which is against their will. Godless men willfully nailed Jesus Christ to the cross and were responsible for their actions, but the entire event was according to the predetermined plan of God. The fall of Satan and the later fall of the human race through Adam and Eve resulted from the creatures' own sin, for which they alone were responsible; yet the events came to pass according to the ordained, predetermined, predestined plan of God. God has decreed a great, eternal purpose for His creation and has ordained every event of history, through which that purpose is being fulfilled. Nothing, not even the fall of man or the death of God's Son, occurs apart from the sovereign decree of God.

> *Oh, the depth of the riches and wisdom and knowledge of God! How unsearchable are His judgments and how inscrutable His ways! "For who has known the mind of the Lord, or who has been His counselor? Or who has given a gift to Him that he might be repaid?" For from Him and through Him and to Him are all things. To Him be glory forever. Amen. (Romans 11:33-36)*

WHAT IS GOD'S ETERNAL PURPOSE IN THE FALL?

Having demonstrated that the fall was the result of the creatures' willful disobedience but that it was also according to the eternal purpose of God, it is now necessary that we endeavor to know that purpose. In light of the evil and suffering that has resulted from the fall, it may seem difficult to accept that there is any good purpose. Nevertheless, God's decree assures us that there is.

We know from the Scriptures that the creation of the universe, the fall of man, the nation of Israel, the cross of Christ, the church, and the judgment of the nations all have one great and overarching purpose—that the fullness of God's attributes might be revealed to His creation so that they might know Him, glorify Him, and fully enjoy Him as God.

THE FULL REVELATION OF GOD'S ATTRIBUTES

God created the universe to be a theater upon which He might display the infinite glory of His person and attributes, that He might be fully known, worshiped, and enjoyed by His creation. It has been said by many that the fall of man is the pitch black sky upon which the stars of God's attributes shine with the greatest intensity of glory. It is only through the fall and the advent of evil that the fullness of God's character may truly be known.

When the Christian worships God, what are the attributes that seem most dear to him? Are they not God's mercy, grace, and unconditional love? Are these not the divine attributes most exalted in all the great hymns of the church? Yet how could these attributes be known except through the fall of man? Unconditional love can only be shown to men who do not meet the conditions of loveliness. Mercy can only be poured forth from the throne of God upon men who deserve condemnation. Grace can only be granted to men who have done nothing to earn it. Our fallenness is of our own doing, and we are obliged to take full responsibility for it. Yet it is through the dark theater of our fallenness that the grace and mercy of God take center stage and shine forth upon an audience of both men and angels. It is in the salvation of fallen man that the wisdom, grace, and mercy of God are revealed—not only to man, but also to every other created being in heaven, earth, and hell (Ephesians 2:7; 3:10).

THE FULL REVELATION OF THE GLORIES OF CHRIST

The greatest work of God is the death and resurrection of the Son of God for the salvation of God's people. However, if man had not fallen, there would have been no Calvary and no Savior. That which now most explains God to us (John 1:18), draws us to Him (John 12:32), and causes us to love Him (I John 4:10, 19) would be unknown to us. What would take its place? What other means could have been used to demonstrate the immeasurable mercies of God? Christ crucified is the great theme of every worthy Christian hymn, sermon, conversation, and thought. Without the fall, redemption would be unknown to us. We would be like the angels, longing to look upon something that we would never and could never experience (I Peter 1:12).

It is wrong and near blasphemy to even hint that the cross of Christ was a mere "Plan B" that was employed only because of Adam's wrong choice in the garden. The cross is the main event to which every other work of God's providence points. All things stand in its shadow. In one sense, the cross was necessary because of the fall; however, in another sense, the fall was necessary so that the glories of God in the cross of Christ might be made fully known!

THE FULL REVELATION OF THE CREATURE'S DEPENDENCE

One of the most awe-inspiring and humbling truths about God is that He is absolutely free from any need or dependence. His existence, the fulfillment of His will, and His good pleasure do not depend upon anyone or anything outside of Himself. He is the only Being who is truly self-existent, self-sustaining, self-sufficient, independent, and free. All other beings derive their life and blessedness from God, but all that is necessary for God's existence and perfect happiness is found in Him.

The existence of the universe requires not only the initial act of creation but also the continued power of God to sustain it. If He were to withdraw His power for even one moment, all would turn to chaos and destruction. This same truth may be applied to the character of moral beings, whether angels or men. Adam in Eden and Satan in heaven, although created righteous and holy, could not stand without the sustaining grace of an Almighty God. How much less are we able to stand, and how much more quickly would we fall without that same sustaining grace? The fall, therefore, provides the greatest example of our constant need for God. If we cannot continue our existence beyond our next breath except for God's preservation, how much less are we able to maintain any semblance of righteousness before Him apart from His grace?

Chapter 4: The Fall of Mankind

BIBLICAL TRUTHS REGARDING THE FALL

The Scriptures affirm three very important truths about the fall of Adam and its devastating effects upon the entire human race. Apart from these truths, it is impossible to account for mankind's moral corruption and the universal presence of evil in a world that was created good. Below are these fundamental truths.

1. **God made Adam to be the representative (or head) of the entire human race.** As head, Adam acted on behalf of all mankind, and the consequences of his actions affect us all.

2. **God imputed Adam's sin to all men.** The words "impute" and "imputation" come from the Latin verb **imputare**, which means, "to consider, reckon, attribute, or charge to one's account." With regard to the fall, it means that God reckons or charges the sin of Adam to every man's account. All men from birth are regarded and treated as sinners on account of Adam's sin. All men bear the guilt and penalty of Adam's sin.

3. **God turned all men over to moral corruption.** The penalty of Adam's sin was not only death but also moral corruption—he fell from his original state of righteousness and became a morally corrupt creature. Since all men bear the guilt of Adam's sin, they also bear the penalty: death and moral corruption. Every one of Adam's descendants is born wholly inclined to evil and at enmity with God.

AN UNDENIABLE FACT, AN UNEXPLAINABLE MYSTERY

The fall of mankind in the fall of Adam will always be shrouded in mystery. It is one of the greatest and most essential doctrines of Christianity, it is clearly asserted in Scripture to be true, and it provides the only adequate explanation for the universal moral corruption of mankind. At the same time, while affirming the doctrine, the Scriptures offer little explanation as to how such things can be so, and no defense is given against the frequent accusations that such things are unjust or unfair. How can it be just for God to impute the sin and guilt of Adam to all of mankind? The following points are worthy of consideration.

1. **The truthfulness of a doctrine is not validated by our ability to comprehend it or reconcile it to our understanding, nor is our inability to do so grounds for rejecting it.** If this were the case, there would be no such thing as Christian doctrine, for there is no revealed truth that does not contain some element of mystery. In Deuteronomy 29:29 the Scriptures declare, "The secret things belong to the Lord our God, but the things that are revealed belong to us and to our children forever, that we may do all the words of this law." It is a great promise of Scripture that the truth we believe and yet do not fully understand will one day be made known to us and that the shadow of uncertainty and doubt that yet remains will disappear in the light of God's full revelation. The Apostle Paul writes in I Corinthians 13:12: "For now we see in a mirror dimly, but then face to face. Now I know in part; then I shall know fully, even as I have been fully known."

2. **Throughout Scripture, God has so proved His perfect justice in His dealings with man that any and every accusation to the contrary is met with a stern rebuke.** "God is greater than man. Why do you contend against Him, saying, 'He will answer none of man's words'?" (Job 33:12b-13). "But who are you, O man, to answer back to God?" (Romans 9:20a). If **God** has made Adam to be the head of the race and imputed his sin to the whole of mankind, it **must** be both just and fair. God has the divine right to purpose and to work according to His own good pleasure.

3. **It was a great demonstration of grace that God would allow one man to be tested on behalf of all other men.** Adam was the fittest and most capable man of the entire human race, and he lived in a place untainted by the sin and corruption that now prevails. God chose the greatest and noblest among us to stand in our place.

4. **All the evidence of Scripture, human history, and the inner witness of conscience points to the certainty that anyone else of Adam's race would have done no better in Adam's place than Adam himself.**

5. **Every person of Adam's race, as soon as he is able, willingly participates in Adam's rebellion against God and so proves that God justly condemns him.**

6. **If it is wrong or unjust for God to condemn the whole human race through the fall of the one man Adam, then it is equally wrong for God to save His people (*i.e.* the redeemed) through the obedience of the one Man Jesus Christ.** If God cannot rightly impute Adam's sin to mankind, then He cannot rightly impute men's sin to Christ or Christ's righteousness to men.

OUR FALL IN ADAM

The declaration, "all men are born in sin," means that God has imputed the sin and guilt of Adam to every one of his descendants. It is important to note that this is not some "theological speculation" or "philosophical construction"; rather, it is the clear teaching of the Scriptures and is validated by every page of human history and by every human life.

In Romans 5:12-19, we find the most important discourse in all of Scripture regarding the fall of Adam and the imputation of his sin to the entire human race. It will therefore serve us well to spend some time studying it. Read the passage until you are familiar with its contents, and then follow the instructions below.

1. Read Romans 5:12 again. Identify the truths that are revealed in the text.

   a. *Just as sin C_____ into the world through one M_____.* The Scriptures affirm that God created all things "good" (Genesis 1:31). The biblical explanation for the presence of sin in God's good world is that it entered or invaded "through" or "by means of" the disobedience of the one man: Adam.

   b. *And D_____ through sin.* Sin entered into the world through Adam's first act of disobedience, and death entered into the world through sin—a devastating chain of events. It is extremely important to note that death did not enter into our world as a "natural consequence" of sin, but as the divine penalty for sin. Death is the punishment or wages of sin (Genesis 2:17; Ezekiel 18:4; Romans 6:23).

c. *So death S_____ to all men.* Having explained how death entered into God's world, Paul affirms what we all know to be true: death has spread to all men. All life inevitably leads to death.

d. *Because A_____ sinned.* Paul's explanation for the spread of death to all men is brief but powerful. Death is the penalty or wage of sin (Roman 6:23), and death has spread to all men because "all sinned." The word "sinned" is written in the aorist tense, which is most commonly used to describe a momentary action in past time or a single event in history. In this case, the historic event to which Paul is referring is the sin and fall of Adam. Considering the grammar and the context (*i.e.* the following verses), this phrase does not mean that death has spread to all men because all men personally "sin" or "have sinned"; rather, it means that death has spread to all men because "all sinned" in that historic moment in the garden when Adam sinned. Through Adam's sin, all were "made sinners" (Romans 5:19). For this reason, the penalty of death has spread to all men, even to infants and the like who die without having committed sin personally.

e. *Explain in your own words the meaning of this verse.*

_____

_____

_____

_____

_____

2. Read Romans 5:13-14 again. Summarize in your own words the meaning of this passage.

_____

_____

_____

_____

_____

_____

NOTES: These verses are given as proof of the fact that all are "made sinners" in Adam. The logic is very clear. According to the Scriptures (Romans 6:23), death is the wage of sin or the penalty for breaking God's law; only sinners or lawbreakers die. Yet countless people died before the Law of Moses was ever given, and countless infants have died in the womb even though they never personally sinned or broke God's law. The death of those who have never personally sinned in the "likeness of the offense of Adam" can only be explained by the fact that the sin of Adam has been imputed to them; they are therefore accounted "sinners" in Adam.

3. Read Romans 5:15-17 again. Identify the truths that are revealed in the passage.

   a. *If many died through one man's T*_____ *(v.15).* The "many" is a reference to the great mass of humanity descended from Adam. Again, Paul is showing that the death experienced by all men is the result of the sin of one man: Adam. Through his transgression, the many "sinned" (5:12); and, therefore, the "many" died.

   b. *The judgment F*_____ *one trespass brought C*_____
   (v.16). The word "judgment" refers to a judicial sentence, decision, or verdict. The word "condemnation" refers to a damnatory sentence or guilty verdict. Adam's transgression resulted in his judgment. His judgment resulted in his condemnation. The penalty for his crime was death. This condemnation and its penalty have been passed on to all men, because "all sinned" in Adam.

   c. *Because of one man's trespass, D*_____ *reigned through that one man (v.17).* Through Adam's one sin, death came to exercise absolute authority over all men (i.e. all men die). Adam's sin was imputed to all men, and all were thereby constituted "sinners." As sinners, all men are under the divine judgment of death.

   d. *Explain in your own words the meaning of these three biblical statements.*

   _____

   _____

   _____

   _____

   _____

   _____

   _____

DISCERNING THE PLIGHT OF MAN

4. Read Romans 5:18-19 again. Identify the truths that are revealed in the passage.

   a. *One trespass led to C_____ for all men (v.18).* This statement simply summarizes what has already been said in verses 12-17. Through the one transgression of Adam, all men were made sinners (vv.12, 19), were condemned (v.16), and were made subject to death (vv.12, 14-15, 17).

   b. *By the one man's D_____ the many were made sinners (v.19).* The word "made" comes from the Greek word **kathístēmi**, which means, "to set down as, declare, or constitute." As a result of Adam's disobedience, all men are now regarded and treated as sinners. It is important to note what the Apostle Paul does **not** say: that as a result of Adam's sin the many were made **sinful** (i.e. born with a sinful nature), which in turn led them to live a life of sin and then to come under the condemnation of death. Rather, Paul states that the many were made **sinners** and brought under the punishment of death even before they had the opportunity to personally sin.

   c. *Explain in your own words the meaning of these two biblical statements.*

_____

_____

_____

_____

_____

PART TWO

THE MORAL DEPRAVITY
AND SINFULNESS OF MAN

Chapter 5: Total Depravity and Moral Corruption

The penalty of Adam's sin was not only death but also moral corruption—he fell from his original state of righteousness and became a morally corrupt creature. Since all men bear the guilt of Adam's sin, they also bear the penalty—death and moral corruption. Every one of Adam's descendants is born morally corrupt, wholly inclined to evil, and under the sentence of death.

It is evident from every individual's experience and the collective experiences of all mankind that man's moral corruption is not a learned or imitated behavior but an inherent trait rooted deeply in the heart. Human history, secular and sacred literature, philosophy, and religion abound with illustrations of man's struggle with his own moral corruption and propensity to evil. The inspired words of the Apostle Paul in Romans 7:15 have been the groan of every man who comes to understand the reality of his own moral corruption: "For I do not understand my own actions. For I do not do what I want, but I do the very thing I hate."

THE MEANING OF "TOTAL DEPRAVITY"

One of the most important phrases used by theologians to describe the depth of man's inherited moral corruption or pollution is the phrase "total depravity." The word "depravity" comes from the Latin preposition **de,** which communicates intensity, and the Latin word **pravus,** which means, "twisted" or "crooked" To say that something is depraved is to say that its original state or form has been thoroughly twisted or perverted. To say that man is depraved is to say that he has fallen from his original state of righteousness and that his very nature has become corrupt. When theologians use the adjectives "total," "pervasive," "holistic," or "radical" when describing man's depravity, it is important to know what they mean and what they do not mean.

What "Total Depravity" Does Not Mean

1. **That the image of God in man was totally lost in the fall.** In Genesis 9:6, I Corinthians 11:7, and James 3:9, the Scriptures still refer to man as having been made in the "image" or "likeness" of God. Therefore, there is a real sense in which the image of God remains in every man.

2. **That man has no knowledge of the person or will of God.** The Scriptures teach us that men know enough of the true God to hate Him, and they know enough of His truth to reject it and attempt to restrain it (Romans 1:18, 30).

3. **That man does not possess a conscience or that he is totally insensitive to good and evil.** Romans 2:15 teaches that all men possess a conscience. If not seared (I Timothy 4:2), such a conscience may lead men to admire virtuous character and actions.

4. **That man is incapable of demonstrating virtue.** There are men who love their families, sacrifice their own lives to save others, and perform great acts of generosity and altruism. It is

recognized that men are capable of loving others, of civic duty, and even of external religious good.

5. **That all men are as immoral or depraved as they could be, that all men are equally immoral, or that all men indulge in every form of evil that exists.** Not all men are delinquents, fornicators, or murderers; but all men are capable of such. The only thing that restrains them is the grace of God.

What "Total Depravity" Does Mean

1. **That the image of God in man has been seriously defaced (or disfigured) and that moral corruption has polluted him entirely.** This truth can be seen clearly in every facet of man's person: body (Romans 6:6, 12; 7:24; 8:10, 13), reason (Romans 1:21; II Corinthians 3:14-15; 4:4; Ephesians 4:17-19), emotions (Romans 1:26-27; Galatians 5:24; II Timothy 3:2-4), and will (Romans 6:17; 7:14-15).

2. **That man is born with a great propensity or inclination toward sin.** All men are capable of the greatest evil, even the most unspeakable crimes and the most shameful perversions.

3. **That all of man's actions are contaminated by his own moral corruption.** Man's moral corruption and sin pervade his most commendable deeds (Isaiah 64:6).

4. **That the deeds of man are not prompted by any love for God or any desire to obey His commands.** No man loves God in a worthy manner or as the law commands (Deuteronomy 6:4-5; Matthew 22:37); nor is there a man who glorifies God in every thought, word, and deed (I Corinthians 10:31; Romans 1:21). All men prefer self to God (II Timothy 3:2-4). All acts of altruism, heroics, civic duty, and external religious good are prompted by the love of self, not the love of God.

5. **That the mind of man is hostile toward God, cannot subject itself to the will of God, and cannot please God (Romans 8:7-8).**

6. **That mankind is inclined to greater and greater moral corruption.** This deterioration would be even more rapid than it is if it were not for the grace of God which restrains the evil of men.

7. **That man cannot free himself from his sinful and depraved condition.** He is spiritually dead (Ephesians 2:1-3), morally corrupt (Psalm 51:5), and unable to change himself (Jeremiah 13:23).

MAN IS BORN IN MORAL CORRUPTION

Now that we have summarized the meaning of total or radical depravity, we will consider more closely the teachings of Scripture. We will find abundant testimony to what we have learned. Since all men bear the guilt of Adam's sin, they also bear the penalty: death and moral corruption. Every one of Adam's descendants is born morally corrupt and inclined to evil.

1. Genesis 5:1-3 clearly shows the devastating consequences of the fall and the spread of moral corruption throughout the human race. Read the text until you are familiar with its contents, and then answer the following questions.

TOTAL DEPRAVITY AND MORAL CORRUPTION

a. *According to Genesis 5:1, in whose image was Adam made?*

_____

_____

_____

b. *According to Genesis 5:3, in whose likeness were Adam's descendants made? Explain the significance of this truth.*

_____

_____

_____

_____

_____

_____

NOTES: Adam was made in the "likeness of God," but the descendants of Adam were made in the fallen and depraved likeness of Adam. It is important to note that men do not inherit Adam's moral corruption in the same way that a son might inherit a physical trait or deformity from his father. The moral corruption of Adam's descendants is a result of God's judgment: Adam sinned and came under the penalty of death and moral corruption. Adam's sin has been imputed to all his descendants; therefore, they are subject to the same penalty—death and corruption.

2. Since the fall of Adam, all men are born with a morally corrupt nature that is deprived of goodness, is hostile toward God, and is inclined to evil. What do the following Scriptures teach about this truth? How do they demonstrate that man's moral corruption is not a learned behavior but a reflection of his very nature?

a. *Psalm 51:5*

_____

_____

_____

_____

_____

> **NOTES:** This does not mean that there was sin in the sexual relations between David's parents that led to his birth. God had commanded that men multiply and bring forth children (Genesis 1:28). David is simply putting forth a truth that is defended throughout the Scriptures and demonstrated in all of human history—man's moral corruption and propensity to evil is not merely a learned behavior but a part of his very being or nature.

b. *Psalm 58:3*

_____

_____

_____

_____

c. *Genesis 8:21*

_____

_____

_____

_____

> **NOTES:** The word "youth" refers to one's early life or childhood. There is no need to teach a child to be selfish or self-centered or to lie or manipulate. Such sinful attitudes and deeds spring forth from his very nature.

3. Having established the truth that all men are born bearing the moral corruption of Adam, we will now consider the Scriptures that illustrate the severity or depth of this moral corruption. What do the following Scriptures teach us about the depth and extent of man's corruption?

a. *Genesis 6:5*

_____

_____

_____

_____

NOTES: To illustrate this point, suppose that one could place on a video all the thoughts of a man—from his earliest moments in childhood to the present day—and then show that film to his closest friends and family, those with whom he had shared his most intimate thoughts and weaknesses. It would be no exaggeration to say that he would be so overcome with shame that he would never be able to face them again.

b. *Job 15:14-16; 25:4-6*

_____

_____

_____

_____

NOTES: The language that is used in both of these texts is extremely strong and offensive. Nevertheless, in their proper contexts, they are true expressions of man apart from the restraining grace of God. We are a fallen race with a malady that can only be cured through redemption in Christ and the regenerating work of the Holy Spirit.

c. *Ecclesiastes 9:3*

_____

_____

_____

_____

_____

d. *Isaiah 64:6*

_____

_____

_____

_____

_____

NOTES: The greatest, most commendable deeds of men are nothing but filthy rags before God. One might clothe a leper in the finest and whitest silk to cover his sores, but the corruption of his flesh would immediately bleed through the garment, leaving it as vile as the man it seeks to cover. In a similar fashion, the best works of men are stained with the corruption of their fallen hearts.

4. When speaking about the moral corruption of man, special attention must be given to the heart. In the Scriptures, the heart refers to the seat of the will and the emotions; it represents the very core of one's being. According to the Scriptures, the very heart of man is corrupt; and from it flows every form of sin, rebellion, and perversity.

    a. *How is the heart of man described in Jeremiah 17:9?*

_____

_____

_____

_____

b. *According to Matthew 15:19-20 and Mark 7:20-23, how does the corrupt heart of man affect all that a man is and does?*

_____

_____

_____

_____

_____

5. To conclude this part of our study on the moral corruption of man, we will consider a brief but powerful statement made by the Lord Jesus Christ in Matthew 7:11. What is this statement, and how does it demonstrate Christ's strong belief in the moral depravity of man?

a. *If you then, who are E_____.*

_____

_____

_____

_____

NOTES: The fact that men may possess sincere affections toward their own and display certain virtues does not disprove the fact that mankind as a whole is a fallen race and that moral corruption pervades the hearts of all. This corruption is so prevalent that Christ may refer to men as ones "who are evil," even in the midst of their good deeds—giving good gifts to their children.

Chapter 6: Spiritual Death

An important phrase used by theologians to describe the depth of man's moral corruption is "spiritual death." According to the Scriptures, the divine judgment that fell upon Adam resulted not only in his physical death but also in his spiritual death. Adam became alienated from God and unresponsive to His will. In turn, he also became responsive to every sort of wicked stimulus, both human and demonic.

The Scriptures teach us that this aspect of the divine judgment that fell upon Adam was not limited to him alone—it includes all mankind. Every human being is born into this world alienated from God, a spiritual stillborn—void of true spiritual life toward God and unresponsive to the person and will of God. In order for fallen man to respond to God in love and obedience, a spiritual resurrection must occur through the supernatural working of God's grace and power.

1. In Genesis 2:17, Adam received a warning from God about the dreadful consequence of disobedience. According to this text, what would occur the day that Adam violated God's command? What does this text teach us about the spiritual death that Adam incurred as the result of his sin?

_____

_____

_____

_____

_____

_____

NOTES: The penalty for Adam's sin was death (Romans 6:23). This death was not only physical but also spiritual. God's warning was not empty. On the very day that Adam ate from the tree of the knowledge of good and evil, he died spiritually—that is, he became alienated from God; unresponsive to His will; and open to every sort of wicked stimulus, both human and demonic.

2. In Ephesians 2:1-3 is found one of Scripture's most revealing descriptions of the spiritual death of fallen man. Read the text several times until you are familiar with its contents. Afterwards, explain in your own words the meaning of each of the following portions.

a. *You were dead in the trespasses and sins (v.1).*

_____

_____

_____

_____

_____

NOTES: Prior to conversion, every person is spiritually dead. The Scriptures consider this spiritual death to be a result of our sin—that is, both the sin imputed to us in Adam (Romans 5:12) and the sin which we ourselves practice (Ephesians 2:2).

b. *In which you once walked, following the course of this world (v.2).*

_____

_____

_____

_____

_____

NOTES: Spiritual death is manifested or made evident by the direction and deeds of a person's life. Prior to conversion, every person "walks in" or "practices" sin as a life-style. By nature, man does not walk according to the will of God, but according to the course of this fallen world—in hostility and disobedience to God.

c. *Following the prince of the power of the air, the spirit that is now at work in the sons of disobedience (v.2).*

_____

_____

_____

_____

_____

_____

> **NOTES:** Prior to conversion, men not only walk in the course of a fallen and disobedient humanity, but they also live in a way that is according to the will and works of the devil. Although most men would deny any allegiance to the devil and would be offended by such an accusation, the Scriptures declare that those who have not been reconciled to God through Christ and regenerated by the Holy Spirit are following the devil's will.

d. _Among whom we all once lived in the passions of our flesh, carrying out the desires of the body and the mind (v.3)._

_____

_____

_____

_____

_____

> **NOTES:** Prior to conversion, every person—without exception—is driven and led by the passions of their flesh (_i.e._ the wicked desires of their fallen humanity, which are rebellious and hostile toward God). They indulge their wicked desires and thoughts.

e. _And were by nature children of wrath, like the rest of mankind (v.3)._

_____

_____

_____

_____

> **NOTES:** Prior to conversion, God's wrath abides upon a person (John 3:36). It is important to understand that the wrath of God is directed toward a person not only

because of what he does, but also because of what he is. Man's fallen and evil nature evokes the wrath of God.

3. In Ephesians 4:17-19 is found another important description of the spiritual death that abides in the heart of every man prior to conversion. Read the text several times until you are familiar with its contents. Afterwards, explain the meaning of each of the following portions.

a. [Fallen men] walk in the futility of their minds. They are darkened in their understanding (vv.17-18).

_____

_____

_____

_____

_____

NOTES: The "minds" of the spiritually dead may be able to accomplish great endeavors in science, architecture, and literature; however, with regard to God, it is empty of truth and filled with all sorts of vanities, heresies, and logical inconsistencies. When fallen men seek to be "spiritual" or "religious," the results are catastrophic or even absurd.

b. Alienated from the life of God (v.18).

_____

_____

_____

_____

_____

c. Because of the ignorance that is in them, due to their hardness of heart (v.18).

_____

_____

_____

_____

_____

NOTES: It is important to understand that man is not a victim, separated from God because of some unavoidable ignorance that he cannot help. Man's ignorance is self-imposed. He is hostile toward God and does not want to know Him or His will. Man is ignorant of spiritual things because he closes his eyes and refuses to look at God and covers his ears and refuses to hear God.

d. *They have become callous and have given themselves up to sensuality, greedy to practice every kind of impurity (v.19).*

_____

_____

_____

_____

_____

NOTES: In hardening his heart against God, fallen man becomes callous to all spiritual truth and virtue. He then voluntarily gives himself over to the very evil that is contrary to God's will and repugnant to His person.

4. In the Scriptures, there are several texts which describe and illustrate what it means to be "spiritually dead." Complete each declaration by filling in the blank, and then write your thoughts.

   a. *Fallen men are D_____ even while they L_____ (I Timothy 5:6).*

   _____

   _____

   _____

   _____

_____

_____

> **NOTES:** Prior to conversion, man is a spiritual corpse—physically alive, but spiritually dead. He is dead to the reality of God and His will.

b. _Fallen men have the reputation of being A_____, but they are D_____ (Revelation 3:1)._

_____

_____

_____

_____

_____

> **NOTES:** Prior to conversion, a man may appear very religious and even God-fearing, but all his works are external and motivated by self-love. In his heart, he does not love God, nor does he seek God's glory.

c. _Fallen men have hearts of S_____ (Ezekiel 11:19)._

_____

_____

_____

_____

> **NOTES:** A statue of stone is inanimate and unresponsive to any sort of stimulus. One can pinch, poke, or prod a statue; but it will not respond. In the same way, the heart of fallen man will not respond to divine stimuli. It is as dead as a stone to God.

d. *Fallen men are like F_____ trees in late autumn, T_____*

dead, U_____ (Jude 12).

_____

_____

_____

_____

_____

NOTES: It would be difficult to find a more graphic illustration of man's spiritual deadness. Prior to conversion, there is no spiritual life whatsoever in man.

e. *Fallen men perform religious duties and rituals that God considers to be D_____ works (Hebrews 6:1; 9:14).*

_____

_____

_____

_____

NOTES: Again, prior to conversion, a man may appear very religious, but all his works are external and motivated by self-love. Though his religious activity may receive the appreciation and applause of men, he is as fruitless as a dead tree before God.

DISCERNING THE PLIGHT OF

Chapter 7: Moral Inability

Part One: The Bondage of Man's Will

THE MEANING OF "MORAL INABILITY"

"Moral inability" is a term that is commonly employed by Bible students to describe the extent of man's moral corruption or total depravity. This doctrine teaches us that fallen man is **unable** to love, obey, or please God.

Upon hearing of such a doctrine, one may ask, "How is man responsible before God if he is **unable** to do anything that God commands?" The answer is very important. If man did not love or obey God because he lacked the mental faculties to do so or was somehow physically restrained, then it would indeed be unfair for God to hold him accountable. Man would be a victim. However, this is not the case. Man's inability is **moral** and stems from his hostility toward God. Man is **unable** to love God because he **hates** God. He is **unable** to obey God because He **disdains** His commands. He is **unable** to please God because he **does not hold the glory and good pleasure of God to be a worthy goal**. Man is not a victim but a culprit. He **cannot** because he **will not**. His corruption and enmity toward God are so great that he would rather suffer eternal perdition than acknowledge God to be God and submit to His sovereignty. For this reason, **moral inability** may also be called **willing hostility**. A wonderfully clear example is found in Genesis 37:4:

> But when [Joseph's] brothers saw that their father loved him more than all his brothers, they hated him and could not speak peacefully to him.

Joseph's brothers "could not speak peacefully to him." This was not because they lacked the physical ability to speak (*i.e.* they were not mute); it was because their hatred was so great toward him that they were unwilling to be friendly to him. In the same way, fallen man's hostility toward God is so great that he cannot bring himself to submit to God.

THE BONDAGE OF MAN'S WILL

Man's will is an expression of his nature. If man possessed a morally pure nature, then his will would be inclined to doing acts that were morally pure. If man were holy and righteous, he would love a holy and righteous God, and he would love and obey His commands. However, fallen man possesses a morally corrupt nature; his will is therefore inclined to do acts that are morally corrupt. Fallen man is unholy and unrighteous; therefore, he hates a holy and righteous God, fights against His truth, and refuses to submit to His commands. Here we find the answer to the often-debated question:

Does man possess a free will?

The Scriptural answer is that man is free to choose as he pleases; but, because his very nature is morally depraved, it always pleases him to turn away from good and choose evil, to hate truth

43

and believe a lie, and to deny God and fight against His will. In one sense, fallen man does have a "free will," but he does not have a "good will." Therefore, he will always "freely" choose in opposition to the person and will of God. Man cannot escape what he is. He is by nature evil, and he does works of evil willfully and freely.

1. In Matthew 7:16-20, we find an excellent illustration of the truth described above, that man's will is an expression of his nature. Read the text several times until you are familiar with its contents, and then explain in your own words the meaning of each verse.

    a. *You will recognize them by their fruits. Are grapes gathered from thornbushes, or figs from thistles? (v.16)*

    _____

    _____

    _____

    _____

    _____

    NOTES: We identify the nature of a tree by the fruit that it bears. In the same way, the true nature or character of a man is revealed not by what he confesses, but by what he does.

    b. *So, every healthy tree bears good fruit, but the diseased tree bears bad fruit (v.17).*

    _____

    _____

    _____

    _____

    NOTES: There is a direct relationship between the nature of a tree and the fruit that it bears. The same is true of a man's nature and his works. A corrupt nature can only produce corrupt works.

c. *A healthy tree cannot bear bad fruit, nor can a diseased tree bear good fruit (v.18).*

_____

_____

_____

_____

_____

NOTES: Here we have one of the greatest examples in the Scriptures of the direct relationship between one's nature and his will. A tree cannot bear fruit **contrary to** its nature; rather, it bears fruit **according to** its nature. Similarly, a man's affections, will, and deeds will always correspond to his nature.

d. *Every tree that does not bear good fruit is cut down and thrown into the fire (v.19).*

_____

_____

_____

_____

NOTES: Jesus is not teaching salvation by works; He is demonstrating the direct relationship between what a person is and what he does. The person who has been saved by faith in Christ has been regenerated by the Holy Spirit. He is a new creature (II Corinthians 5:17) with new affections for God and for His will. He has become a good tree who bears good fruit. His works are not intended (or able) to save him; instead, they are the **evidence** of God's saving work in him.

e. *Thus you will recognize them by their fruits (v.20).*

_____

_____

_____

_____

_____

> **NOTES:** This text begins (v.16) and ends (v.20) with the same phrase: "You will recognize them by their fruits." The repetition emphasizes two important truths: (1) there is an undeniable and direct relationship between the nature and the will; and (2) our confession is not sufficient evidence of genuine conversion without good fruit that we bear throughout our lives.

2. In Matthew 12:34-35 is found another excellent illustration of fallen man's moral inability. Read the text several times until you are familiar with its contents, and then write your thoughts on each of the following phrases.

   a. *You brood of vipers! How can you speak good, when you are evil? (v.34)*

   _____

   _____

   _____

   _____

> **NOTES:** We would be hard pressed to find a greater example of moral inability than that which is found here in Jesus' rebuke of the Pharisees. They **could not** speak what is good because they **were** evil. They bore bad fruit because they were bad trees (Matthew 7:17).

   b. *For out of the abundance of the heart the mouth speaks (v.34).*

   _____

   _____

   _____

   _____

NOTES: In the Scriptures, there is always a direct relationship between a man's heart and his affections, thoughts, words, and works. Man wills, speaks, and acts in accordance with his nature.

c. *The good person out of his good treasure brings forth good, and the evil person out of his evil treasure brings forth evil (v.35)*

_____

_____

_____

_____

_____

NOTES: This is a powerful parallel to Matthew 7:17-18: "So, every healthy tree bears good fruit, but the diseased tree bears bad fruit. A healthy tree cannot bear bad fruit, nor can a diseased tree bear good fruit."

Chapter 8: Moral Inability

Part Two: The Impotence of Man's Mind and Heart

In the preceding chapter, we considered the relationship between the nature and the will. In doing so, we also discovered that, since he is born with a morally corrupt nature, man cannot (because he will not) respond positively to the person or works of God. In this chapter and the next, we will consider many of the most important "cannot" passages in the Scriptures—the texts which clearly show the moral inability of fallen man in every aspect of his being.

FALLEN MAN CANNOT KNOW THE THINGS OF GOD

Through God's gracious providence, the human race has gained great intellectual achievements in science, technology, medicine, and so forth. Nevertheless, fallen man's knowledge of God is nothing more than a twisted maze of heresy and futile thinking. This ignorance is not the result of a "hidden God," but of a "hiding man." God has clearly revealed Himself to men through creation, His sovereign works in history, the Scriptures, and finally through His incarnate Son. Man, being spiritually dead and morally corrupt, has responded to this revelation by closing his eyes and covering his ears. He **cannot** know the truth, because he hates it and seeks to repress it. He hates the truth because it is God's truth, and it speaks against him. Therefore, he cannot bear it.

1. According to I Corinthians 2:14, can fallen man understand the things of God taught by the Holy Spirit? Explain your answer.

_____

_____

_____

_____

_____

_____

NOTES: Fallen man cannot understand the things of God. The things of God are spiritually discerned, while fallen man is spiritually dead. For this reason, he rejects the knowledge of God as foolishness. In order for a man to understand, appreciate, and accept the knowledge of God; he must be regenerated by the Holy Spirit. Jesus told Nicodemus in John 3:3, "Truly, truly, I say to you, unless one is born again he cannot see the kingdom of God."

2. In the first part of our study on moral inability, we learned that man cannot love God because of his hostility toward Him. Now we will see that man's hostility toward God is also reflected in his opposition to God's truth. It is important to understand that men are not helpless victims who genuinely desire spiritual truth but cannot obtain it. On the contrary, they hate the truth and do all that is in their power to deny and repress it! What do the following Scriptures teach us about this truth?

a. *Job 21:14-15*

_____

_____

_____

_____

_____

b. *Romans 1:18*

_____

_____

_____

_____

_____

NOTES: The word "suppress" comes from a Greek word **katéchō**, which may also be translated, "to restrain, hinder, detain, or hold back."

DISCERNING THE PLIGHT OF MAN

3. In Romans 1:21-32 is found an important description of humanity's hostility toward God and His truth. It demonstrates that fallen man is not a victim, who desires the truth of God but does not have the faculties to know it. Rather, he is a "hater of the truth," who does not want to know it. Read the text several times, especially focusing on verses 21-25. Afterwards, explain in your own words the meaning of the following portions.

a. *For although they knew God, they did not honor Him as God or give thanks to Him (v.21).*

_____

_____

_____

_____

_____

_____

NOTES: Unbelief in God is not an intellectual problem, but a moral one. According to the Scriptures, there are no atheists. God has clearly revealed Himself to all men, but men suppress this knowledge so that they might continue in their unrighteousness and prideful autonomy.

b. *But they became futile in their thinking, and their foolish hearts were darkened (v.21).*

_____

_____

_____

_____

_____

NOTES: Having rejected the knowledge of God, unbelieving humanity begins its descent into intellectual and moral darkness.

c. *Claiming to be wise, they became fools (v.22).*

_____

_____

_____

_____

_____

d. *And exchanged the glory of the immortal God for images resembling mortal man and birds and animals and creeping things (v.23).*

_____

_____

_____

_____

_____

NOTES: The madness of unbelieving men is most revealed in the objects of their worship. Throughout history, we see men rejecting the Creator who is above them and worshiping creatures who are below them. Their self-worship degrades into the worship of even the lowliest creatures.

e. *Because they exchanged the truth about God for a lie (v.25).*

_____

_____

_____

_____

_____

_____

> **NOTES:** Man's core problem is his depraved nature, which is hostile toward the righteous and holy God. This hostility leads man to suppress the truth of God in exchange for a completely distorted view of reality. The only alternative to the truth of God is a lie (see verse 18).

f. *And worshiped and served the creature rather than the Creator, who is blessed forever (v.25).*

_____

_____

_____

_____

_____

> **NOTES:** Man was created to worship and serve the God who made him—the God of all perfections, who is infinitely worthy of his love and allegiance. When he sins, man exchanges this privilege for worship of corruptible self and birds and animals and creeping things (verse 23).

FALLEN MAN CANNOT LOVE GOD

Most, even the irreligious, claim some degree of love or affection toward God; and very rarely would we ever encounter an individual so bold as to confess their "hatred" toward Him. Nevertheless, the Scriptures testify that fallen man **cannot** love God. In fact, all of Adam's race **hates** God and lives at war against Him. Most who claim a genuine love for God know very little about His attributes and works as they are revealed in the Scriptures; therefore, the "god" they love is nothing more than a figment of their imagination. They have made a "god" in their own image, and they love what they have made. God declares in Psalm 50:21, "You thought that I was one like yourself; but now I rebuke you."

If fallen men who claim to love God were to investigate the Scriptures, they would most certainly find a God much different from the object of their affections. If they went on to study the attributes of God (such as holiness, justice, sovereignty, and wrath), they would most likely respond in disgust and declare (as many have), "My God's not like that!" or "I could never love a God like that!" We would quickly see that when fallen man is confronted with the true God of the Scriptures, his only reaction is hatred and hostility! What is the reason for this adverse reaction? Again, it has to do with who man is at the very core of his being. If man were by nature holy and righteous, then he could easily love a holy and righteous God and would joyfully submit to His laws. However, man is by nature depraved and corrupt, so he cannot!

1. In the Scriptures, a name has great significance and communicates something about the person who bears it. What names are attributed to fallen man in the following Scriptures? What do they communicate to us about his moral corruption and hostility toward God?

   a. H_____ of God (Romans 1:30).

   _____

   _____

   _____

   _____

   _____

   NOTES: This phrase comes from the Greek word ***theostugês*** [***theós*** = God + ***stúgō*** = to hate]. It refers to a hater, despiser, or disdainer of God.

   b. E_____ of God (Romans 5:10).

   _____

   _____

   _____

   _____

   _____

   NOTES: This word comes from the Greek word ***echthrós***. It denotes an adversary who is at enmity with another, hostile toward another, or opposed to another.

2. Why would any rational creature hate the very God who brought it into existence and self-lessly sustained it? Why does fallen man hate God and live at enmity against Him? What do the following Scriptures tell us? Match each truth with its corresponding text(s) by placing the correct letter in each blank.

_____ *Romans 8:7*

a. *Fallen man hates God because he loves evil and is engaged in evil deeds. He does not come to God because he fears that his evil deeds might be exposed.*

_____ *John 3:19-20; Colossians 1:21*

b. *Fallen man hates God because he loves sinful pleasures rather than God.*

_____ *II Timothy 3:4*

c. *Fallen man hates God because his mind is depraved and set on the flesh (i.e. it is morally corrupt and strongly desires the very things that a holy and righteous God opposes).*

DISCERNING THE PLIGHT OF

Chapter 9: Moral Inability

Part Three: The Impotence of Man's Strength

FALLEN MAN CANNOT SEEK GOD

We live in a world full of self-proclaimed "seekers of God," yet the Scriptures destroy all such boasting with one simple declaration: "No one seeks for God" (Romans 3:11). Quite often, we hear young converts to Christianity begin their testimony with the words, "For years I was seeking after God." But the Scriptures again reply, "There is none who seeks for God." Man is an utterly fallen creature, whose nature is depraved and perverse. He hates God and opposes His truth because it convicts him of his depravity and rebellion. He will not come to God; in fact, he will attempt to do absolutely everything in his power to escape from Him and forget about Him. God is righteous; man is a lawbreaker. Man is therefore no more inclined to seek God than a criminal at large is inclined to seek an officer of the law! If someone does genuinely seek God, it is only because God is working in his life and drawing him to Himself.

1. Often we hear men claim to be "seekers of the truth" or "seekers of God." How do the following Scriptures respond to such claims?

   a. *According to Romans 1:18, does fallen man sincerely seek the truth?*

   _____

   _____

   _____

   _____

   > **NOTES:** The word "suppress" comes from the Greek word ***katéchō***, which may also be translated, "to restrain, hinder, detain, or hold back."

   b. *According to Romans 3:11 does fallen man sincerely seek God?*

   _____

   _____

_____

_____

_____

> **NOTES:** The word "seeks" comes from the Greek word ***ekzētéō*** [***ek*** or ***ex*** = from, out of + ***zētéō*** = to seek]. It may also be translated, "to seek out, inquire, or carefully search out."

2. We have learned that fallen man will not seek God. Why does man have such an aversion to God? Why will fallen man not seek Him? What does John 3:19-20 teach us?

_____

_____

_____

_____

_____

3. The Scriptures teach us that fallen man will not (and therefore cannot) seek God. According to the teachings of Jesus in John 6:44 and John 6:65, what must happen before a man can seek God and His salvation?

_____

_____

_____

_____

_____

> **NOTES:** The word "draws" in verse 44 comes from the Greek word ***hélkō***, which means, "to drag, draw, or haul." Greek scholars Louw & Nida give this meaning to the word: "To drag or pull by physical force, often implying resistance—to draw, to lead by force."[4] To be clear, God does not draw men to Himself by dragging them against their will; rather,

---

[4] *Greek-English Lexicon of the New Testament*, 15.178

He first regenerates the hearts of men, giving them a new nature. This new nature, which has been recreated in the image of God, possesses new and righteous affections that then draw these men irresistibly to Christ.

FALLEN MAN CANNOT OBEY OR PLEASE GOD

There is one great common denominator among those religions outside of Christianity: they all believe that a right standing with God is based upon obedience, personal merit, or some ability to please God. Christianity stands alone in declaring that man is hopelessly and helplessly lost on his own. He cannot improve his standing before God, he cannot obey God, and he cannot please God. If he is to be saved, God alone must save him! It is this one truth that fallen man hates most of all, for it requires him to humble himself before God, acknowledge his own sin, and ask for mercy!

1. In Romans 8:7-8 is one of the most important descriptions of man's moral inability in the Scriptures. Read the text several times until you are familiar with its contents, and then explain its meaning. What does each of the following phrases teach us about man's inability to obey or please God?

   a. *For the mind that is set on the flesh is hostile to God (v.7).*

   _____

   _____

   _____

   _____

   NOTES: The "mind that is set on the flesh" refers to the mind of anyone who is still in an unconverted state, unregenerate, and without Christ.

   b. *For it does not submit to God's law; indeed, it cannot (v.7).*

   _____

   _____

   _____

   _____

> **NOTES:** The reason for fallen man's inability to be subject to God's law is moral. He has the necessary revelation and faculties to know God and submit to Him. However, his love for unrighteousness and his desire for autonomy make submission impossible.

c. *Those who are in the flesh cannot please God (v.8).*

_____

_____

_____

_____

> **NOTES:** The phrase, "in the flesh," refers to anyone who is still in an unconverted state, unregenerate, and without Christ. The word "please" comes from the Greek word *aréskō*, which may also be translated, "gain approval." Fallen man, apart from Christ, cannot gain God's approval.

FALLEN MAN CANNOT CHANGE OR REFORM HIMSELF

The twentieth century began with great optimism with regard to man's ability to evolve into a greater, nobler creature. It was supposed to be the age of reform, but it ended in a stupor of despair and confusion. The Scriptures clearly teach that man is born spiritually dead and morally depraved. Any and every human effort to reform is hopeless. Any and every attempt to make oneself pleasing or acceptable to God will end in utter failure. Man has only one hope: the mercy and grace of God.

1. Having established man's inability to love God or to seek Him, we will now consider what the Scriptures teach about man's inability to change, reform himself, or make himself right before God. What do the following Scriptures teach us about this truth?

    a. *Job 9:29-31*

    _____

    _____

    _____

    _____

b. *Job 14:4*

_____

_____

_____

_____

c. *Jeremiah 2:22*

_____

_____

_____

_____

d. *Jeremiah 13:23*

_____

_____

_____

_____

SUMMARY

Man is born in sin with a corrupt nature that is hostile to God and His will. Furthermore, he cannot reform himself or make himself in any way acceptable to God. The plight of man is utterly hopeless apart from the mercies of God. God alone is able to reconcile man to Himself through the atoning work of Jesus Christ and to transform him through the regenerating work of the Holy Spirit. The way of salvation for humanity is not through autonomy, self-reliance, or self-reform; it is through a return to God through His Son Jesus Christ.

Chapter 10: Enslavement to Satan

Before we go on to study the character and universality of sin, it is important that we consider fallen man's relationship to Satan. We will see that fallen man is not only alienated from God but also united to Satan in his hostility toward God and rebellion against Him.

In the beginning, Adam was free to obey God and exercise dominion over all the earth. As a result of his rebellion against God, both he and his race fell into corruption and slavery. Since the fall, every son and daughter of Adam is born in bondage to sin and enslaved to Satan. Although few men would ever regard themselves to be "followers" of the devil, the Scriptures testify that all men are born under his dominion and held captive by him to do his will. Although it is proper to use the term "enslavement," we must understand that man is not a victim held against his will. Fallen man is a culprit who has rejected the rule of God and given himself over to the rule of Satan.

THE RULE OF SATAN

We must be very careful whenever we speak about the rule and power of Satan. God and the devil are **not** equal powers locked in some cosmic struggle to win the universe. The devil is a finite creature, whom God created and over whom God rules with absolute sovereignty. Although Satan's rebellion against God is his own doing, it has been ordained and permitted by God for His own purposes and glory.

Without denying or diminishing the truth of God's absolute sovereignty, we can say that there is a very real sense in which this present fallen world and its fallen inhabitants lie in the power of the evil one. The Scriptures bear abundant testimony to this truth.

1. In Luke 4:5-6, Satan makes a declaration about himself and his relationship to this fallen world. What does he declare, and what does it mean?

_____

_____

_____

_____

_____

NOTES: It is important to note two things. First, Jesus did not contest the devil's claim; there is a real sense in which Satan has dominion in this world. Second, as he boasts, Satan states that this domain had been "delivered" to him. The devil's rule is both permitted and limited by God.

2. It is important to understand that Satan's declaration in Luke 4:6 is no idle boast. What does I John 5:19 teach us about this truth?

_____

_____

_____

_____

_____

_____

NOTES: The Scriptures declare that this fallen world and its fallen inhabitants are held firmly in the devil's grip. Fallen man seeks to gain independence from God, and in so doing he unwittingly makes himself a slave to Satan. This is a frightening truth.

3. In the Scriptures, a name is important in that it often communicates something about the person who bears it. What are the names or titles given to Satan in the following Scriptures?

   a. *The R_____ of this W_____ (John 12:31; 14:30; 16:11).* God is the absolute Sovereign over all things, but there is a real sense in which dominion has been given to Satan to rule over this fallen world. With such a ruler, is there any wonder why this present age is filled with such evil and why fallen man suffers such misery?

   b. *The G_____ of this W_____ (II Corinthians 4:4).* It is the sure testimony of Scripture that there is only one true God. Satan is here called the "god of this world" only in the sense that he is working with power in this present evil age; fallen men have made him their "god" and live according to his will.

   c. *The P_____ of the P_____ of the A_____ (Ephesians 2:2).* Satan is a spirit; as such, he is unhindered by the material restraints that bind man. His power and authority go far beyond any earthbound prince.

SATAN AND FALLEN MAN

Both Satan and man are fallen creatures, and there is great affinity between them (*i.e.* they have much in common). They are alike in their moral corruption and in their enmity against God. Although this fact is repulsive to most, it is nevertheless true. There is such a moral likeness between fallen man and Satan that, prior to conversion, all men are considered to be not only Satan's subjects but also his children.

1. We have learned from our study of the Scriptures that Satan is described as both a ruler and a god over Adam's fallen race and that he works effectively among them. How is fallen man described in the following Scriptures? Fill in the blanks, and then write your thoughts.

   a. *Fallen man is a C_____ of the D_____ (I John 3:8-10; see also John 8:44).*

   _____

   _____

   _____

   _____

   NOTES: The Scriptures deny the universal fatherhood of God (*i.e.* that God has taken all men to be His children); rather, Adam's race is divided into two categories. There are **the children of the devil**, who refuse God's offer of mercy and remain in their rebellion against Him. They show themselves to be children of the devil in that they practice the sinful works of their father, the devil. And there are **the children of God**, who receive God's forgiveness and adoption as sons through the atoning death of Jesus Christ. They show themselves to be the children of God in that they practice the righteous works of their heavenly Father.

   b. *Fallen man lives under the P_____ of S_____ (Acts 26:18; see also Colossians 1:13).*

   _____

   _____

   _____

   _____

   NOTES: The word "power" refers to the power, authority, dominion, or jurisdiction of Satan. To live under Satan's dominion is to live under his rule or government.

c. *Fallen man F_____ the P_____ of the power of the air (Ephesians 2:2).*

_____

_____

_____

_____

_____

NOTES: The word "following" comes from the Greek preposition **katá**, which in this context denotes agreement, accordance, or conformity. The title, "prince of the power of the air," communicates two important truths: (1) Satan has a measure of sovereignty over humanity; and (2) Satan is a spirit, unhindered by the material restraints that bind man. His power and authority go far beyond any earthbound prince.

d. *Fallen man is caught in the S_____ of the D_____ (II Timothy 2:26).*

_____

_____

_____

_____

NOTES: A snare or noose is a type of trap that was used in ancient times to catch birds and other animals. It was a hidden device that would entangle an animal unexpectedly and suddenly. It serves as an excellent illustration of Satan's deadly work.

e. *Fallen man is C_____ by the devil to do his W_____ (II Timothy 2:26).*

_____

_____

DISCERNING THE PLIGHT OF MAN

_____

_____

_____

NOTES: Satan captures men in order to enslave them and use them to carry out his will in this fallen world. Once again, it is important to note that man is not an unwilling victim of the devil; rather, he is a lawbreaking culprit who through disobedience has aligned himself with the devil.

2. We have learned from our study of the Scriptures that Satan is described as both a ruler and a god over Adam's fallen race. According to the following Scriptures, how does he work among fallen man? How is it that he makes them his subjects and enslaves them to do his will? Consider the following Scriptures, and write your thoughts on the listed methods.

    a. _Satan masks his true identity (II Corinthians 11:14-15)._

    _____

    _____

    _____

    _____

    _____

    NOTES: Throughout human history, countless theological errors and cults have been started by those who have discarded God's Word and propagated teachings that they supposedly received from voices, visions, dreams, or angelic visitations.

    b. _Satan lies and deceives (John 8:44; Revelation 12:9)._

    _____

    _____

    _____

_____

_____

_____

NOTES: Jesus taught that knowledge of the truth sets men free (John 8:32). Therefore, it is no wonder that twisting the truth into a lie is Satan's most common and powerful weapon to bring men into slavery and death.

c. *Satan blinds men to the truth (II Corinthians 4:4).*

_____

_____

_____

_____

_____

NOTES: Satan's dominion is one of darkness, ignorance, moral corruption, and death. He blinds those in rebellion against God through deceit, confusion, vanity, and pride. This blindness can only be taken away by the light of the gospel and the illuminating work of the Holy Spirit. Jesus came to give sight to the blind (Luke 4:18). The Apostle Paul's ministry was "to open [men's] eyes, so that they may turn from darkness to light and from the power of Satan to God, that they may receive forgiveness of sins and a place among those who are sanctified by faith in [Christ]" (Acts 26:18).

d. *Satan tempts (Matthew 4:3; I Thessalonians 3:5).*

_____

_____

_____

NOTES: Satan tempts men and is therefore referred to as the "tempter." The word "tempt" comes from the Greek word *peirázō*, which means, "to tempt, try, or test." When the word is used with regard to God's dealings with men, it always denotes testing or trying and has the purpose of revealing what is in the heart of men and leading them to greater sanctification. James writes, "Let no one say when he is tempted, 'I am being tempted by God,' for God cannot be tempted with evil, and He Himself tempts no one" (James 1:13). When the word is used with regard to Satan, however, it denotes temptation with the purpose of causing men to sin. It is important to note that when a man falls by means of temptation he has neither grounds for excuse nor room to pass the blame to Satan. Each man is responsible for his own actions and bears the blame for them. James continues in verse 14, "But each person is tempted when he is lured and enticed by his own desire."

Chapter 11: The Character and Universality of Sin

THE SINFULNESS OF SIN

To begin our study of man's personal participation in Adam's rebellion, we must have a correct understanding of the nature or character of sin. Therefore, it is necessary that we study the many attributes and manifestations of sin as they are revealed in the Scriptures. In doing this, we will discover that sin is much more than an error in moral judgment or even than disobedience to some impersonal law. Sin is a crime against the person of God. In our study, we must do more than simply define terms; we must regain a biblical understanding of the *sinfulness of sin*. We live in a world and worship in churches that, for the most part, no longer understand the heinous nature of sin; therefore, we must endeavor to rediscover what has been lost. Our understanding of God and of the greatness of our salvation in Christ depends upon it.

SIN IS ALWAYS AGAINST GOD

Sin is always first and foremost against God and an affront to His person. To disobey a divine command is to clench the fist and wag it in the face of the One who gives life to all and rules over all. Today, if people speak of sin at all, they speak of sin against man, sin against society, or even sin against nature; but rarely do we hear of sin against God. A person is thought to be good if he has good relations with his fellow men, even if he lives with total disregard for God and His will. It is often asked how God can judge an atheist who is a good man, but this shows a blindness to the fact that any man who denies His Creator and renders nothing to the One who gives him all things cannot be good. The Scriptures record that King David lied to his people, committed adultery, and even orchestrated the murder of an innocent man. Yet, when confronted with his sins, he cried out to God, "Against You, You only, have I sinned and done what is evil in Your sight" (Psalm 51:4). David knew that all sin is first and foremost against God. Until one understands this truth, he can never understand the heinous nature of sin.

SIN IS FAILURE TO LOVE GOD

The greatest of all sins is the violation of the greatest of all commands: "And you shall love the Lord your God with all your heart and with all your soul and with all your mind and with all your strength" (Mark 12:30). Christ declared, "If you love Me, you will keep My commandments" (John 14:15). Therefore, all disobedience is a demonstration of a lack of love toward God. For this reason, when the Apostle Paul sought to prove the depravity of mankind in the first three chapters of the book of Romans, he referred to Adam's race as "haters of God" (Romans 1:30). No greater indictment could be made against fallen man. A lack of love for God is at the very heart of all rebellion. Additionally, a man may be very religious and conscientious of divine law and duty, yet he will still be found a terrible sinner before God if his obedience is prompted by anything other than love for God.

Sin Is Failure to Glorify God

The Scriptures declare that man was created for the glory of God and that all that man does, even the most menial tasks of eating and drinking, should be done for God's glory (I Corinthians 10:31). To glorify God is to esteem the worth of God above all things; to delight in God; to be satisfied in God; and to live before God with the reverence, gratitude, and worship that is due Him. Sin is the very opposite of glorifying God. When man sins, he becomes the opposite of what he was created to be. A sinful man is a creature who has dislocated himself and perverted the very reason for his existence. He has replaced God with self and God's will with self-determination. The Apostle Paul writes, "Although they knew God, they did not honor Him as God," and they "exchanged the truth about God for a lie and worshiped and served the creature rather than the Creator, who is blessed forever" (Romans 1:21, 25). Sin's roots go much deeper than what is seen on the surface. Sin is man's refusal to acknowledge God's right as God. Sin is man's determination to set himself above his Creator, usurp His throne, and steal His glory. Sin is fundamentally a refusal to glorify God as God, and it manifests itself whenever man seeks his own glory above God's.

Sin Is Godless and Ungodly

The word "godlessness" denotes a refusal to acknowledge God as God and a desire to live a "godless" existence, free from His sovereignty and law. The word "ungodliness" denotes a refusal to be conformed to the character and will of God and a desire for moral depravity instead of likeness to God. It has been said that the greatest compliment that may be paid to another man is to express a desire to be **with him** and to be **like him**. Sin reveals an inward desire to live **without God** and to be **unlike God**. This is a great affront to God!

Sin Is Rebellion and Insubordination

In I Samuel 15:23, the Scriptures declare, "For rebellion is as the sin of divination, and presumption is as iniquity and idolatry." The word "rebellion" is translated from the Hebrew word **meri**, which means, "to be contentious, rebellious, or disobedient toward." The word "presumption" is translated from the Hebrew word **patsar**, which literally means, "to press or push." It denotes one who is pushy, insolent, arrogant, and presumptuous. There are no small sins, because all sin is rebellion and insubordination. To practice any form of rebellion is as evil as partaking in some pagan or demonic ritual. To practice any form of insubordination is as evil as partaking in gross iniquity or rendering worship to a false god.

Sin Is Lawlessness

In I John 3:4, the Scriptures declare, "Everyone who makes a practice of sinning also practices lawlessness; sin is lawlessness." The word "lawlessness" is translated from the Greek word **anomía** [a = without, no + **nómos** = law]. To practice "lawlessness" is to live "without law" or as though God had never revealed His will to mankind. A person may "practice lawlessness" by openly defying the rule and law of God or by simply being unconcerned and willingly ignorant. In either case, the person is showing contempt for God and His law.

Sin Is Treachery

The word "treachery" denotes a deceitful and unfaithful act against another. Throughout the Scriptures, treachery is an element found in all sin (Ezekiel 18:24), in rebellion (Isaiah 48:8), in forsaking the true God for idols (I Chronicles 5:25), and in any form of apostasy or turning away from God (Psalm 78:57). All sin is a betrayal of the One who created us and lovingly sustains our lives.

Sin Is an Abomination

Sin, more than anything else, is an abomination to God. An abomination is a foul, disgusting, abominable thing, detestable and loathsome to God and an object of His hatred (Proverbs 6:16). In the Scriptures, all sin is an abomination, and to sin is to act abominably (Ezekiel 16:52). Proverbs 28:9 declares, "If one turns away his ear from hearing the law, even his prayer is an abomination." Proverbs 15:8-9 declares that the lifestyle and sacrifice of the wicked are abominations to God. All idolatry (Deuteronomy 7:25) and all acts of injustice (Deuteronomy 25:16) are abominations before the Lord; so is any person who is devious (Proverbs 3:32; 15:26), a liar (Proverbs 12:22), perverse in heart (Proverbs 11:20), or proud in heart (Proverbs 16:5). In Revelation 21:8, 27, the Scriptures conclude with the warning that the abominable and those who practice abominations will suffer eternal punishment.

Sin Is Missing the Mark

The most common Hebrew word for sin in the Old Testament is **chata**, which means, "to miss the mark, miss the way, or go wrong." It is used in Judges 20:16 when relating that the men of Benjamin could sling a stone at a hair and not "miss." It is also used in Proverbs 19:2 to warn that he who hurries his footsteps "misses his way" or "errs" (NASB). In the New Testament, the most common Greek word for sin is **hamartánō**, which may also be translated, "to miss the mark, err, be mistaken, or wander from the path." According to the Scriptures, the mark or goal toward which man is to aim is the will of God. Any thought, word, or deed that does not conform to God's will is sin. It is important to note that sin (**chata** or **hamartánō**) is never seen as an innocent mistake or honest error; rather, it is always a willful act of disobedience resulting from man's moral corruption and rebellion against God.

Sin Is Transgressing the Boundary

In the Old Testament, the word "transgress" is translated from the Hebrew word **abar**, which means, "to cross or pass over, to pass through, or to bypass." To transgress God's command is to go beyond what is permitted by His commands; it is to ignore the restrictions imposed upon us by God's law and to run beyond its fence. In the New Testament, the word "transgress" is translated from the Greek word **parabaínō**, which means, "to go by the side of, to go past, to pass over, or to step over." In Matthew 15:2-3 is found an excellent example of the idea of **parabaínō**. The Pharisees asked Jesus, "Why do Your disciples break [**parabaínō**] the tradition of the elders? For they do not wash their hands when they eat." Jesus responded, "And why do you break [**parabaínō**] the commandment of God for the sake of your tradition?"

THE UNIVERSALITY OF SIN

Now that we have seen something of the sinfulness of sin, we must turn our attention to one of the most important doctrines in all the Scriptures—**the universality of sin**. Sin is not a rare or unusual phenomenon confined to a small minority of the human race; it is universal in its scope. The Scriptures are clear that "all have sinned and fall short of the glory of God" (Romans 3:23). There is not one member of Adam's race that has not joined him in the rebellion he began. Those who would deny such a truth must deny the testimony of Scripture; of human history; and of their own sinful thoughts, words, and deeds.

1. In Romans 3:23 is found one of the most important passages in all the Scriptures with regard to the sinfulness and disobedience of all men. What does this passage teach us?

_____

_____

_____

_____

_____

NOTES: The word "sinned" comes from the Greek word **hamartánō**, which may also be translated, "to miss the mark, err, be mistaken, or wander from the path." The verb phrase, "fall short of the glory of God," is probably a reference to man's constant failure to do all things for God's praise, honor, and good pleasure. The Apostle Paul writes elsewhere, "For although they knew God, they did not honor Him as God" (Romans 1:21).

2. The Scriptures are filled with innumerable references to the sinfulness and willing disobedience of man against God and His will. What do the following Scriptures teach us about the universal disobedience of all men?

   a. *I Kings 8:46*

_____

_____

_____

_____

NOTES: The word "sin" comes from the Hebrew word *chata*, which means, "to miss the mark, miss the way, or go wrong."

b. *Psalm 143:2*

_____

_____

_____

_____

NOTES: The word "righteous" comes from the Hebrew word *tsadeq*, which means, "to be just or righteous." In the Scriptures, the person and will of God is the standard for all righteousness. To be righteous is to be conformed to God's character and will.

c. *Proverbs 20:9*

_____

_____

_____

_____

NOTES: The word "sin" comes from the Hebrew word *chata* (see definition above).

d. *Ecclesiastes 7:20*

_____

_____

_____

_____

> **NOTES:** The word "righteous" comes from the Hebrew word **tsaddiq**, which denotes one who is righteous, just, or blameless. The verb "sins" comes from the Hebrew word **chata** (see definition above).

e. *Isaiah 53:6*

_____

_____

_____

_____

_____

> **NOTES:** Here we not only hear the divine verdict concerning man's sinfulness, but we also see the only possible remedy: the Messiah carrying man's sin, suffering the wrath of God, and dying in man's place (vv.4-5, 10).

3. In Romans 3:9-12 is found a collection of Old Testament quotes ordered by the Apostle Paul to demonstrate humanity's universal sinfulness and willing disobedience against God. Read the text several times until you are familiar with its contents. Afterwards, write your thoughts on each portion below.

   a. *What then? Are we Jews any better off? No, not at all. For we have already charged that all, both Jews and Greeks, are under sin (v.9).*

_____

_____

_____

_____

_____

b. *As it is written: "None is righteous, no, not one" (v.10).*

_____

_____

_____

_____

_____

NOTES: The word "righteous" comes from the Greek word ***díkaios***, which denotes that which is just, right, blameless, or innocent. Like its Hebrew counterpart (***tsaddiq***), it carries the idea of being conformed to the nature and will of God.

c. *"No one understands; no one seeks for God" (v.11).*

_____

_____

_____

_____

NOTES: We must remember that this lack of understanding is directly linked to man's rebellion and insubordination. Man is willfully ignorant of God because he suppresses the truth (Romans 1:18) and does not desire to know His ways (Job 21:14-15). The reason man does not seek God on His terms is found in John 3:19-20.

d. *"All have turned aside; together they have become worthless" (v.12).*

_____

_____

_____

_____

_____

> **NOTES:** The phrase "turned aside" comes from the Greek word ***ekklínō***, which may also be translated, "bend away, deviate, or pervert." The word "worthless" is translated from the Greek word ***achreióō***, which denotes someone or something that has become unprofitable or worthless.

e. *"No one does good, not even one"* (v.12).

_____

_____

_____

_____

_____

> **NOTES:** This is a powerful indictment against any and all who believe that a right standing before God can be achieved by personal merit.

4. The testimony of Scripture against all men is contrary to popular humanistic belief in the inherent goodness of man. For this reason, many today reject the biblical view of man in favor of a more positive opinion. What warning is given in I John 1:8-10 to those who would oppose the biblical testimony against man and insist that they are not sinners?

_____

_____

_____

_____

_____

GOD'S DISPOSITION TOWARD THE SINNER

Chapter 12: Grief

GOD'S DISPOSITION TOWARD THE SINNER

The Scriptures teach that God is the holy and righteous Judge of His creation. Although He is compassionate and gracious, slow to anger, and abounding in lovingkindness, He will by no means leave the guilty unpunished (Exodus 34:6-7). When the holiness, righteousness, and love of God are challenged by the depravity and open rebellion of man, the result is divine judgment.

King Solomon declared in Ecclesiastes 7:29, "See, this alone I found, that God made man upright, but they have sought out many schemes." This change in man must inevitably result in a change in God's disposition toward man. Man was created "upright" and was a source of great satisfaction to God. This satisfaction is seen in God's declaration that the creation of man was "good" (Genesis 1:31) and in the many blessings that He conferred upon man (Genesis 1:26-30). With the advent of sin, God's disposition was changed: joy turned into grief, favor turned into wrath, satisfaction turned into abhorrence, and peace turned into enmity.

Throughout the ages, God continues to be "compassionate and gracious" toward a rebellious humanity. "He makes His sun rise on the evil and on the good, and sends rain on the just and on the unjust" (Matthew 5:45). In the fullness of time, He sent His Son to die for the sins of the world in order to provide reconciliation and peace to all who might believe (John 1:29; II Corinthians 5:19). Finally, the Scriptures testify that God stretches out His hands "all the day" to offer salvation to a "disobedient and contrary people" (Isaiah 65:2; Romans 10:21). Though all of this is true in the fullest sense, nevertheless, we must not deny or ignore the teaching of Scripture with regard to **God's disposition** toward the wicked. In this part of our study, we will consider this aspect of God's character and works.

GRIEF

Can an all-sufficient and all-powerful God suffer or experience grief? While we must affirm that the God of the Scriptures is self-determining (*i.e.* His disposition and actions are not governed by the disposition and actions of others) and immutable in His perfections (*i.e.* He does not change), we must equally hold to the truth that He is not apathetic or unmoved by His creature's response to Him. He truly feels, loves, hates, grieves, and is capable of entering into personal relationships.

When the Scriptures speak about God's grief, it is always in the context of man's sin. God grieves over the sin and rebellion of His creatures. This grief is the result of the offensiveness of sin to His holy person and of the destruction, misery, and loss that it brings upon His creation.

1. In Genesis 6:6, we find one the greatest teachings in Scripture regarding God's reaction to the sinfulness and rebellion of His creatures. Write your thoughts on this passage. What does it teach us?

_____

_____

_____

_____

_____

NOTES: The word "grieved" comes from the Hebrew word **atsab**, which denotes hurt, pain, or grief. The phrase "to His heart" is what theologians refer to as an **anthropomorphism**—the ascribing of human or physical characteristics to God in order to reveal something about Him. God is spirit and does not possess an actual heart. The phrase simply communicates to us that God was truly and deeply grieved. It is important to note that this text does not teach us that God changed His mind about creating man or that He recognized an error in doing so; rather, it simply shows that man's rebellion grieved Him. What had been a source of joy became a source of grief, because of sin.

2. We will now consider three other very important passages in the Old Testament that refer to God grieving over the sins of men. What do these texts teach us? Write your thoughts.

   a. _Psalm 78:40_

   _____

   _____

   _____

   _____

   _____

   _____

   NOTES: This is a reference to Israel's wandering in the wilderness, which was a result of refusing to enter into the land of Canaan after being redeemed from the bondage of Egypt. The word "grieved" comes from the Hebrew word **atsab** (see definition above).

   b. _Isaiah 63:10_

   _____

   _____

_____

_____

_____

_____

NOTES: The word "grieved" comes from the Hebrew word **atsab** (see definition above). This text finds a New Testament parallel in Ephesians 4:30.

c. *Ezekiel 6:9*

_____

_____

_____

_____

_____

_____

NOTES: The word "broken" is translated from the Hebrew word **shabar**, which means, "to break, break in pieces, shatter, or demolish." It provides us with a vivid picture of the extent of God's grief due to the sins of His people.

3. In the New Testament is found an important text with regard to God's grief over man's sinfulness and rebellion against Him. Write your thoughts on Ephesians 4:30. What does it teach us?

_____

_____

_____

_____

DISCERNING THE PLIGHT OF MAN

> **NOTES:** The word "grieve" comes from the Greek word *lupéō*, which can also be translated, "to make sorrowful, sadden, hurt, or distress."

4. It is important for us to understand that sin is portrayed in Scripture not only as a thing that grieves God, but also as something that is a burden to Him. What do the following Scriptures teach us about this truth?

   a. *Isaiah 43:24*

   _____

   _____

   _____

   _____

> **NOTES:** The word "burdened" comes from the Hebrew verb *abad*, which means, "to work or labor." It is often associated with the idea of putting someone into servile labor or laying a burden upon a slave. The word "wearied" comes from the Hebrew verb *yaga*, which means, "to toil," "to be weary," or "to wear out." It is important to understand that God is not weakened by our sin, nor is His power diminished. Figurative language is being used to illustrate how the sins of man grieve (or burden) the heart of God.

   b. *Amos 2:13*

   _____

   _____

   _____

   _____

> **NOTES:** The phrase "press you down" is translated from the Hebrew word *uq*, which means, "to crush or cause to totter as though under the weight of something." Again, figurative language is being used to illustrate how the sins of man grieve the heart of God.

DISCERNING THE PLIGHT OF MAN

Chapter 13: Wrath

Part One: The Nature of God's Wrath

When the holiness, justice, and love of God meet the depravity, injustice, and lovelessness of man; the inevitable result is divine anger, indignation, and wrath. The word translated "wrath" in the Old Testament comes from three different Hebrew words: **qetsep** (wrath, anger, indignation); **hema** (wrath, anger, disgust, displeasure, fury, rage, heat, poison); and **'aph** (which literally means, "nostril" or "nose"). This last word came to denote anger in that the flaring of the nostrils is a sign of anger. In the New Testament, the word "wrath" is translated from two different Greek words: **orgê** (wrath, anger) and **thumós** (anger, indignation, passion, rage, wrath). In the Scriptures, divine wrath refers to God's holy displeasure and righteous indignation directed toward the sinner and his sin.

In speaking of the wrath of God, it is important to understand that it is not an uncontrollable, irrational, or selfish emotion; rather, it is the result of His character and a necessary element of His government. Because of God's nature and character, He must react adversely to sin. **God is holy**; therefore, He is repulsed by evil and breaks fellowship with the wicked. **God is love** and zealously loves all that is good; such intense love for righteousness manifests itself in an equally intense hatred of all that is evil. **God is righteous**; therefore, He must judge wickedness and condemn it. God's holiness, love, and righteousness cause Him to hate sin and to come with terrible and often violent wrath against it. If man is an object of God's wrath, it is because he has chosen to challenge God's sovereignty, violate His holy will, and expose himself to judgment.

Today, many reject the doctrine of divine wrath or any similar teaching that would even suggest that a loving and merciful God could be wrathful or that He would manifest such wrath in the judgment and condemnation of sinners. They argue that such ideas are nothing more than the erroneous conclusions of primitive men who saw God as hostile, vengeful, and even cruel. As Christians, we should reject any doctrine that would portray God as cruel or ignore His compassion. Nevertheless, we must not forsake the Scriptures' clear teaching on the doctrine of divine wrath and punishment. There are more references in the Scriptures to the anger and wrath of God than there are to His love, kindness, and compassion. God *is* compassionate and gracious, slow to anger, and abounding in lovingkindness; yet He *will* punish unrepentant sinners in order to administer justice among His creatures and vindicate His holy name.

1. Before we proceed any further in our study of the wrath of God, it is extremely important that we understand the holy and righteous nature of God's wrath. Though man's wrath is often the result of sinful passions, the wrath of God is a manifestation of His righteousness and holiness.

    a. *According to Romans 1:18, why does the wrath of God fall upon man?*

    _____

    _____

_____

_____

_____

> **NOTES:** The word "suppress" comes from the Greek word **katéchō**, which may also be translated, "to restrain, hinder, detain, or hold back." Here we see that the revelation of God's wrath is not a capricious act, but the righteous response of a holy God to the unrighteousness of man.

b. *According to Exodus 15:7, what about God is revealed in every manifestation of His wrath? Answer the question by filling in the blanks; then explain the meaning of this verse.*

   (1) The G_____ of His M_____.

   _____

   _____

   _____

   _____

   _____

> **NOTES:** The word "majesty" is translated from the Hebrew word **gaon**, which also denotes exaltation, glory, majesty, excellence, and eminence. The wrath of man is often a revelation of some flaw or weakness in his character. In contrast, God's wrath is a revelation of His perfections—His holiness, righteousness, and love.

2. According to the Scriptures, the wrath of God is so intense that it cannot be comprehended or resisted. What do the following texts teach us about this truth?

   a. *Psalm 90:11*

   _____

   _____

   _____

_____

_____

> **NOTES:** The word "considers" comes from the Hebrew word **yada**, which means, "to know." The idea is that no one has known the full extent of God's wrath toward the wicked. Even the most powerful demonstrations of His wrath (*e.g.* Sodom and Gomorrah or the global flood) were only limited revelations or examples. The phrase, "according to the fear of You," denotes that man's fear of God ought to be in accordance with or in proportion to the greatness of God's wrath. However, no man knows God's wrath as it truly is; therefore, no man fears God as he truly ought.

b. *Jeremiah 10:10*

_____

_____

_____

_____

c. *Jeremiah 23:19-20*

_____

_____

_____

_____

d. *Nahum 1:6*

_____

_____

DISCERNING THE PLIGHT OF MAN

_____

_____

_____

_____

> **NOTES:** The questions are rhetorical, and the answers are obvious. No one individually, nor the entire creation collectively, can stand before the wrath of God.

3. It is important to understand that the wrath of God is not limited to the Old Testament Scriptures; it is also clearly presented in many Scriptures of the New Testament. What do the following New Testament passages teach us about the wrath of God?

    a. _Romans 2:5-6_

    _____

    _____

    _____

    _____

    _____

> **NOTES:** The phrase "storing up" comes from the Greek word _**thēsaurízō**_, which literally means, "to store up treasure." Through their disobedience, men store up wrath like treasure. The "day of wrath when God's righteous judgment will be revealed" refers to the end of the age and the universal judgment of all men.

    b. _Ephesians 5:3-6; Colossians 3:5-6_

    _____

    _____

    _____

    _____

> **NOTES:** The primary idea put forth in both of these texts is the absolute certainty of the wrath of God that will one day come upon the wicked. Sinners often deny the reality of divine judgment and wrath, and they also mock these doctrines and those who proclaim them (see II Peter 3:3-4).

4. From the Scriptures, it is clear that God is a God not only of love and mercy but also of wrath and vengeance. God's holiness, love, and righteousness cause Him to hate sin and to come with terrible and violent vengeance against it. If man challenges God's sovereignty and violates His will, then he will expose himself to His wrath. According to the following Scriptures, how should all men respond to this truth?

   a. *Psalm 76:7*

   _____

   _____

   _____

   _____

   _____

   b. *Psalm 90:11-12*

   _____

   _____

   _____

   _____

5. Even though the reality of the wrath of God is undeniable, we should also understand that He is merciful. God takes no pleasure in the death of the wicked; rather, He often delays His wrath and gives the sinner ample opportunity to turn away from his sin. Nevertheless, those who continue in rebellion will most certainly face the wrath of God. What does Exodus 34:6-7 teach us about this truth?

_____

_____

_____

_____

_____

_____

NOTES: Here we see the mercy of God revealed in His forgiveness of the repentant and believing, and we see the righteous judgment of God revealed in His punishment of the unrepentant and unbelieving. The reference to the children and grandchildren is qualified in Exodus 20:5 by the phrase "of those who hate Me." God's judgment falls upon the descendants who continue in the hatred of their forefathers.

Chapter 14: Wrath

Part Two: Biblical Descriptions of God's Wrath

In the previous chapter, we looked at several Scriptures from the Old and New Testaments in order to gain a biblical understanding of the nature of God's wrath. In this chapter, we'll continue to study the wrath of God, focusing on some of the language the Scriptures use to describe it.

1. How is God described in Nahum 1:2? What do these descriptions communicate to us about God? Write your thoughts.

   a. *The Lord is avenging and W_____.*

   _____

   _____

   _____

   _____

   _____

   NOTES: The word "wrathful" is translated from the Hebrew phrase ***ba'al chemah***. The word ***ba'al*** refers to an owner, possessor, or lord. The word ***chemah*** denotes heat, rage, anger, and wrath. Combined, the words literally mean, "a possessor of hot or burning wrath."

   b. *The Lord K_____ W_____ for His E_____.*

   _____

   _____

   _____

   _____

   _____

DISCERNING THE PLIGHT OF MAN

> **NOTES:** The word "wrath" is translated from the Hebrew word *chemah* (see above). The word "keeps" is translated from the Hebrew word *natar*, which may also be translated, "to keep or hold." The idea of wrath being reserved or stored is also revealed to us in the New Testament. In Romans 2:5-6, the Apostle Paul declares: "But because of your hard and impenitent heart you are storing up wrath for yourself on the day of wrath when God's righteous judgment will be revealed. He will render to each one according to His works."

2. It is important to understand that the description of God as avenging and wrathful is not confined to the Old Testament. How is God described in the following Scriptures from the New Testament? Explain the meaning of these descriptions.

a. *The God who I_____ W_____ (Romans 3:5).*

_____

_____

_____

_____

> **NOTES:** The word "inflict" is translated from the Greek word *epiphérō*, which means, "to bring upon or against another." The word "wrath" is translated from the Greek word *orgē*, which denotes wrath or anger. Divine wrath is not merely a natural consequence for sinful actions; the Scriptures teach that God is **active** in bringing His righteous wrath upon the unrepentant sinner.

b. *The God who is a C_____ F_____ (Hebrews 12:29).*

_____

_____

_____

_____

> **NOTES:** Fire is often used throughout the Scriptures to describe the wrath of God. It is one of the most terrifying forces in nature. The word "consuming" comes from the Greek word *katanalískō*, which means, "to use up or spend." The wrath of God burns up all that is in its path until it is utterly used up, spent, or consumed. In Exodus 15:7,

Moses declares, "You send out Your fury; it consumes them [*i.e.* the wicked] like stubble." This should be a terrifying thought for the unrepentant sinner!

3. Throughout the Scriptures, several different terms are used to describe the wrath of God. It is necessary for us to consider the meaning of these terms so that we might have a better understanding of divine wrath.

   a. *According to the following Scriptures, identify the terms that are used to describe the wrath of God.*

      (1) F_____ (Exodus 15:7). This comes from the single Hebrew word **charon**, denoting burning, fierceness, and fury. The NASB translates this word as "burning anger."

      (2) H_____ D_____ (Deuteronomy 9:19). This phrase comes from the single Hebrew word **chema**, denoting heat, rage, anger, and wrath.

      (3) I_____ (Psalm 7:11). This word, from the Hebrew word **zaam**, communicates intense anger.

      (4) W_____ (Psalm 90:11). From the Hebrew verb **ebrah**, this means, "to pass over or overflow." The wrath of God is like a raging river, overflowing its banks and carrying away all that is in its path. The NASB translates this as "fury."

      (5) The F_____ A_____ of the Lord (Jeremiah 30:24). The phrase is translated from two Hebrew words. The first is **charon**, denoting burning, fierceness, or fury. The second is **'aph**, which literally means, "nostril" or "nose." The word came to denote anger in that the flaring of the nostrils is a sign of anger.

   b. *Explain in your own words what these terms communicate to us about the wrath of God.*

      _____

      _____

      _____

      _____

      _____

      _____

      _____

4. Throughout the Scriptures, we find many metaphors that are employed to communicate the fierce nature of God's wrath against the sinner and his sin. Below, we will consider a few of the most important metaphors.

   a. *According to the Scriptures given, identify the metaphors that are used to describe the wrath of God.*

   (1) A F_____ that devours (Deuteronomy 32:22).

   (2) A whetted (or sharpened) S_____ (Psalm 7:12).

   (3) A fiery A_____ (Psalm 7:13).

   (4) A W_____ T_____ (Jeremiah 30:23).

   (5) An O_____ F_____ (Nahum 1:8).

   (6) A G_____ W_____ (Revelation 14:19; see also Isaiah 63:2-6).

   b. *Explain in your own words what these metaphors communicate to us about the wrath of God.*

   _____

   _____

   _____

   _____

   _____

5. In Psalm 7:11-13 is found a very revealing description of the wrath of God as it is manifest against sin. Read the text several times until you are familiar with its contents, and then write your thoughts. What does this text teach us about the wrath of God?

   _____

   _____

   _____

   _____

   _____

NOTES: There are several important truths we learn from the text. *First*, God's indignation is a result of His righteousness, not some imperfection in His character. *Second*, God's indignation is the result of man's continued rebellion. God is "merciful and gracious, slow to anger, and abounding in steadfast love" (Exodus 34:6-7). He will pardon the repentant sinner, but the unrepentant sinner makes himself an object of God's wrath. *Finally*, God purposefully and actively comes against the sinner with His wrath. The sinner's suffering is more than merely the natural consequences of sin; it is the result of God's active judgment.

Chapter 15: Hatred or Abhorrence

Closely related to the wrath or anger of God is His hatred or abhorrence of both sin and the sinner. Two other words that are used in association with this divine disposition toward sin are "detest" and "loathe."

A popular statement often used in contemporary Christianity is, "God loves the sinner but hates the sin." Although in one sense this statement is true, it is also very misleading, because it only reads one side of the coin—it only declares one half of the truth. There is a real sense in which God loves the sinner and is benevolent toward him. However, there is another equally real sense in which the sinner is the object of God's wrath, holy displeasure, detestation, loathing, abhorrence, and hatred. The Scriptures teach us that God does not hate and abhor sin alone; rather, this disposition also extends toward those who practice sin. We must understand that it is impossible to separate sin from the sinner. God does not punish sin; He punishes sinners. It is the man who practices sin, not the sin itself, that is condemned to the wrath of God in hell.

It is undeniable that the Scriptures use words such as "abhorrence" and "hatred" to describe God's disposition toward unrepentant sinners. Therefore, it is imperative that we correctly understand the truth that is being communicated. We shall now consider several helpful points.

First, we must understand the reality of the hatred of God. Webster's Dictionary defines "hate" as "a feeling of extreme enmity toward someone; to regard another with active hostility or to have a strong aversion toward another; to detest, loathe, abhor, or abominate." Although these are hard and harsh words, most (if not all) are used in the Scriptures to describe God's relationship to sin and the sinner. *Second*, we must understand that God's hatred exists in perfect harmony with all of His other attributes. Unlike man's hatred, God's hatred is holy and just. In fact, God's abhorrence of evil—and of those who practice it—is the result of His holiness, righteousness, and love. God loves all that is upright and good with the greatest intensity; correspondingly, He hates all that is perverse and evil with equal intensity. Consider this truth: we are fallen creatures; yet, when we read of the Holocaust of Nazi Germany, we cannot remain neutral—we burn with a righteous indignation, abhorrence, and loathing, not only against the heinous crimes that were committed, but also against those who committed them. How much more will the supremely righteous and holy God, who considers sin to be infinitely wicked, abhor and even loathe both the sin and the sinner! *Third*, we must understand that the truth of God's wrath and hatred toward the sinner is not a denial of His love. Because of God's holiness, righteousness, and justice; His wrath abides upon the unrepentant sinner (John 3:36), He is angry with the wicked every day (Psalm 7:11), and He hates all who do iniquity (Psalm 5:5). Nevertheless, His love is of such a nature that He is able to be benevolent, gracious, and merciful to those who are the very objects of His hatred and to work on their behalf for their salvation. God's holiness and righteousness burns against the sinner. Yet with one hand His mercy holds back His wrath, and with the other He beckons the sinner to be reconciled through the gospel. *Fourth*, we must understand that God's hatred will have an ultimate manifestation. Although God's mercy holds back His wrath and extends an olive branch of peace to the sinner, there will come a time when He will withdraw His offer, and reconciliation will no longer be possible. At that moment, all that will be left for the unrepentant sinner is the terrifying manifestation of the wrath and holy hatred of God against the wicked. Sinful men should consider this truth with fear and trembling.

1. What does Psalm 5:4-5 teach us about God's disposition toward sin and the unrepentant sinner?

_____

_____

_____

_____

_____

_____

NOTES: God takes no pleasure or delight in sin because He is inherently, perfectly, and infinitely holy and righteous. He cannot be tempted by sin (James 1:13), nor can He bear sin to be in His presence, as it is an abomination to Him. It is because of His holiness and righteousness that His hatred is manifested toward all those who practice iniquity. The word "hate" is translated from the Hebrew verb **sane**. The verb and its derivatives have the root meaning, "to hate." "It expresses an emotional attitude toward persons and things that are opposed, detested, despised and with which one wishes to have no contact or relationship. It is therefore the opposite of love. Whereas love draws and unites, hate separates and keeps distant. The hated and hating persons are considered foes or enemies and are considered odious, utterly unappealing."[5]

2. Psalm 5 is not alone in attesting to the holy hatred of God against sin and the unrepentant sinner who practices it. Psalm 11:4-7 is another very important text concerning God's hatred. What does this passage teach us? Write your thoughts on each of the following portions.

    a. _The Lord is in His holy temple; the Lord's throne is in heaven (v.4)._

_____

_____

_____

_____

_____

---

[5] R. Laird Harris, Gleason L. Archer, Jr., and Bruce K. Waltke; _Theological Wordbook of the Old Testament_, 2272b

NOTES: Two great truths are communicated to us about God here: (1) He is holy, and (2) He is absolutely sovereign over all creation.

b. *His eyes see, His eyelids test the children of man. The Lord tests the righteous (vv.4-5).*

_____

_____

_____

_____

NOTES: Two more great truths are communicated to us about God here: (1) He is omniscient—nothing is hidden from His eye or beyond His knowledge; and (2) He examines the thoughts, words, and actions of men in order to recompense them according to their deeds.

c. *But His soul hates the wicked and the one who loves violence (v.5).*

_____

_____

_____

_____

NOTES: In this Psalm, the sinner is described as "the wicked" (vv.5, 6) and the "one who loves violence" (v.5), and he is contrasted with the "upright" (v.7). The hatred of God is not confined only to those who do physical violence; it is active toward all who practice sin and are contrary to God's righteousness. The word "hates" is translated from the Hebrew verb **sane** (see definition above, under Main Point 1). The reference to God's "soul" is an anthropomorphism—ascribing a human characteristic to God in order to communicate a truth about Him. When a man does something with all his heart or soul, it means that he is doing it with the greatest intentionality and intensity. Therefore, the truth being communicated here is that God hates or abhors the wicked with the greatest intentionality and intensity.

d. *Let Him rain coals on the wicked; fire and sulfur and a scorching wind shall be the portion of their cup (v.6).*

_____

_____

_____

_____

NOTES: This is a clear and accurate description of the wrath of God against the wicked. The strongest metaphors of calamity and destruction cannot even begin to describe the judgment of God that will fall upon the wicked. Even the fiery destruction of Sodom and Gomorrah is but a limited description of God's wrath (Genesis 19:24-25).

e. *For the Lord is righteous; He loves righteous deeds; the upright shall behold His face (v.7).*

_____

_____

_____

_____

NOTES: Here is revealed the reason for God's intense hatred manifested toward the wicked: He is righteous and loves righteousness. If God truly loves righteousness with the greatest intensity, He will abhor evil deeds and evil men with equal intensity.

3. We will now consider six passages of Scripture that employ the words "detest," "loathe," or "abomination" (or their derivatives). Our purpose is to gain a deeper understanding of God's holy hatred toward sin and the sinner. Carefully read each text, and write your thoughts. What do these verses teach us?

   a. *Leviticus 20:23*

   _____

   _____

_____

_____

> **NOTES:** The word "detested" comes from the Hebrew verb **quts**, which communicates repulsion, loathing, detestation, abhorrence, or sickening dread. This intense reaction was the result of the idolatrous nations' sinful practices.

b. *Deuteronomy 18:12*

_____

_____

_____

> **NOTES:** The word "abomination" comes from the Hebrew word **toebah**, which may also be translated, "detestable" or "loathsome." The unrepentant sinner is detestable to the Lord because his deeds are detestable to the Lord.

c. *Deuteronomy 25:16*

_____

_____

_____

> **NOTES:** The word "abomination" comes from the same Hebrew word as in the passage above: **toebah**. The unrepentant sinner is abominable to the Lord because he acts unjustly.

d. *Psalm 95:10*

_____

_____

NOTES: The word "loathed" comes from the Hebrew verb **quts** (see definition above). The objects of God's loathing here are the Israelites, who perished in the wilderness because of their unbelief and rebellion (verse 11).

e. *Titus 1:16*

_____

_____

_____

_____

NOTES: The word "detestable" comes from the Greek word **bdeluktós**, which is derived from the word **bdéō**, which means, "to stink." It denotes that which is detestable, abhorrent, nauseating, or abominable. Once again, it is the sinner's moral corruption and disobedience to God's will that make him detestable.

f. *Revelation 21:8*

_____

_____

_____

_____

NOTES: The word "detestable" comes from the Greek word **bdelússō**, which is derived from **bdéō** (see definition above). Here we see the final destination of those unrepentant sinners who make themselves objects of God's hatred: the lake of fire and second death.

Chapter 16: Enmity and Vengeance

To conclude our study of God's disposition toward the sinner, we will consider two important terms that are not often used by contemporary Christians, but are commonly used in the Scriptures to describe God's reaction to the moral corruption and disobedience of man: enmity and vengeance.

ENMITY

We often hear about sinful man's unceasing war against God, but little is taught about God's unceasing war against the wicked. The hostility between God and the sinner is not one-sided; it is mutual. The Scriptures clearly teach that God considers the sinner to be His enemy, that God has declared war on the wicked. The sinner's only hope is to drop his weapon and raise the white flag of surrender before it is forever too late.

1. In Nahum 1:2 is found a reference to the enmity that God has toward the sinner and the judgment that accompanies it. Identify how the sinner is described in this text, and then write your thoughts.

   a. *The Lord takes vengeance on His A_____.*

   _____

   _____

   _____

   _____

   > **NOTES:** The word comes from the Hebrew word **tsar**, which may also be translated, "enemy" or "foe."

   b. *He keeps wrath for His E_____.*

   _____

   _____

   _____

   _____

NOTES: The word is derived from the Hebrew verb **ayab**, which means, "to be hostile to, as toward an enemy, foe, or adversary."

2. Another important Old Testament reference to the enmity of God against the sinner is found in Isaiah 63:10. This verse not only demonstrates the enmity of God against the sinner, but it also reveals the reason for such enmity. Read the text, and write your thoughts.

_____

_____

_____

_____

NOTES: The phrase, "to be their enemy," comes from the Hebrew verb **ayab** (see definition above).

3. In Romans 5:10 is found one of the most important references in the Scriptures to the enmity of God against the sinner. It also demonstrates that this doctrine is not limited to the Old Testament, but it reaches the New Testament as well. Write your thoughts on this passage.

_____

_____

_____

_____

NOTES: The word "enemies" comes from the Greek word **echthrós**, which denotes an enemy—one who is hostile or in opposition to another. It is sometimes held that man is the enemy of God, but that God is never the enemy of man. This statement, however, is quite misleading. In this verse, both ideas are present; but the reader should keep in mind that the sinner's opposition to God is only secondary—the primary thought of the text is God's holy opposition to the sinner.

VENGEANCE

Closely related to the wrath of God is His vengeance. In the Scriptures, the desire for vengeance is often presented as a vice of wicked men (Leviticus 19:18; I Samuel 25:25, 30-33); therefore, it is difficult for us to understand how a holy and loving God could be a ***God of vengeance***. What we must understand is that God's vengeance is always motivated by His zeal for holiness and justice.

Today, many reject the doctrine of divine vengeance or any teaching that would even suggest that a loving and merciful God could be vengeful. They argue that such ideas are nothing more than the erroneous conclusions of primitive men who saw God as hostile and cruel. As Christians, we should reject any doctrine that would portray God as cruel or ignore His compassion. Nevertheless, we must not forsake the clear teaching of Scripture on the doctrine of divine vengeance. God is compassionate and gracious, slow to anger, and abounding in lovingkindness; but He is also just. He will punish the sinner with the purpose of vindicating His name and administering justice among His creatures. In light of man's sin, God is ***right*** to avenge Himself. Three times in the book of Jeremiah, God asks, "Shall I not punish them for these things? And shall I not avenge Myself on a nation such as this?" (Jeremiah 5:9, 29; 9:9).

1. In the Scriptures, a name carries great significance and communicates something about the one who bears it. What name or title is given to God in Psalm 94:1? What does it reveal to us about Him?

    _____

    _____

    _____

    _____

    _____

NOTES: The word "vengeance" is translated from the Hebrew word ***nequama***, which may be translated, "vengeance" or "revenge." The repetition of the title communicates the certainty of what is being said about God. He is a God of vengeance, who will certainly avenge the wrong that has been done against His person, His law, and His creation.

2. How is God described in Nahum 1:2? Explain the meaning of these descriptions. What do they communicate to us about God?

    a. *The Lord is a J_____ and A_____ God.*

    _____

    _____

_____

_____

_____

> **NOTES:** The word "jealous" comes from the Hebrew word **quano**, which communicates a strong desire or even zeal to possess or maintain possession of something or someone. The word "avenging" is derived from the Hebrew word **naqam**, which means, "to avenge or take vengeance." The idea communicated is that God is jealous for His own honor. He will not share His glory with another (Isaiah 42:8), nor will He allow it to be depreciated by sinful men through their idolatry or disobedience. He will take vengeance upon the unrepentant sinner who dishonors Him.

b. _The Lord takes V_____ on His A_____._

_____

_____

_____

> **NOTES:** The phrase "takes vengeance on" comes from the Hebrew word **naqam**, and it could also be translated, "avenges" or "exacts punishment on." The word "adversaries" comes from the Hebrew word **tsar**, which may also be translated, "enemy" or "foe." Through his disobedience, the sinner makes God his enemy and opens himself up to God's vengeance or punishment.

3. In Deuteronomy 32:39-42 is found one of the most terrifying illustrations of God's vengeance against those who despise His authority and violate His law. Read the passage carefully, and then write your thoughts on each of the following portions.

   a. _See now that I, even I, am He, and there is no god beside Me (v.39)._

   _____

   _____

   _____

NOTES: God here declares His supremacy over all creation. He is the only true God, and He is the Creator and Sustainer of all. He is therefore (1) worthy of man's worship, thanksgiving, and obedience; and (2) right in requiring these things from man.

b. *I kill and I make alive; I wound and I heal; and there is none that can deliver out of My hand (v.39).*

_____

_____

_____

_____

NOTES: God here declares His sovereignty over all creation. He is man's inescapable reality. This was the great lesson taught to Nebuchadnezzar, king of Babylon, who after great humiliation declared, "All the inhabitants of the earth are accounted as nothing, but He does according to His will among the host of heaven and among the inhabitants of the earth; and none can stay His hand or say to Him, 'What have You done?'" (Daniel 4:35).

c. *If I sharpen My flashing sword and My hand takes hold on judgment, I will take vengeance on My adversaries and will repay those who hate Me. I will make My arrows drunk with blood, and My sword shall devour flesh—with the blood of the slain and the captives (vv.41-42).*

_____

_____

_____

_____

NOTES: These are two of the most terrifying verses in all the Scriptures. As God's love for the repentant sinner is incomprehensible, so is His wrath for the unrepentant sinner. Consider two important truths: (1) obstinate disobedience is a manifestation of the sinner's hatred or disdain of God; and (2) God's wrath will one day be poured out in its fullness upon those who remain unrepentant. The wicked will be devoured like a wax figurine before a blast furnace.

4. We will now consider two more Old Testament Scriptures that give us greater insight into the reality and meaning of God's vengeance against the sinner and his sin. Write your thoughts on each passage.

   a. *Deuteronomy 7:9-10*

   _____

   _____

   _____

   _____

   b. *Isaiah 1:24*

   _____

   _____

   _____

   _____

   > **NOTES:** The word "relief" comes from the Hebrew word ***nacham***, which may also be translated, "consoled." We have considered God's reaction in the face of man's rebellion—grief, anger, and abhorrence. Now we see that in pouring out His wrath and satisfying the demands of His justice, God is found to be relieved or consoled.

5. The doctrine of divine vengeance is not limited to the Old Testament; it is clearly taught in the New Testament as well. Whenever God's holiness and justice are confronted with man's rebellion, the result is wrath and vengeance. What does Hebrews 10:30-31 teach us about this truth?

   _____

   _____

   _____

   _____

   _____

PART FOUR

GOD'S JUDGMENT
OF THE SINNER

DISCERNING THE PLIGHT OF

Chapter 17: Separated from God

Having considered God's disposition toward the unrepentant sinner, we will now consider the actual judgments that result from sin. There are many today who avoid the doctrine of divine judgment, and there are others who deny it altogether. However, if we believe the Scriptures to be the inspired Word of God, we must accept this doctrine with the same conviction as other doctrines. God is the Judge of all the earth (Genesis 18:25), and He will punish the wicked according to their dues.

We will begin our study with possibly the greatest and most foundational of all judgments: *separation* or *estrangement* from God.

IMPLICATIONS OF THE SINNER'S SEPARATION FROM GOD

As physical death is the separation of the soul from the body, spiritual death is the separation of the soul from God. God is morally perfect and separated from all evil. It is impossible for Him to take pleasure in sin or to join in fellowship with those who practice unrighteousness. Therefore, man's moral corruption and unrighteousness stand as a great wall between himself and God and make fellowship with God impossible. Unless this sin is taken out of the way, man is destined to live and die outside of God's fellowship and be cut off from the fullness of His blessing.

We can begin to comprehend how devastating this result of sin is to humanity when we consider its implications alongside the following truths about God.

God is the Author of all life, both physical and spiritual: To be estranged from God, therefore, is to be estranged from life itself.

God is the Source of all knowledge and light: To be estranged from God, therefore, is to be given over to ignorance and darkness.

God is the Wellspring of infinite glory, value, and wonder: To be estranged from God, therefore, is to be united to all that is base, worthless, and mundane.

God is the Standard of all that is right and good: To be estranged from God, therefore, is to be turned over to all that is unrighteous, perverted, and evil.

God is the Reason for man's existence: To be estranged from God, therefore, is to be separated from purpose and meaning and to be given over to futility and hopelessness.

1. Having considered the blessedness of God and the negative implications of being separated from Him, write your thoughts. What are the benefits that nearness to God brings? What are the consequences of being separated from Him?

_____

_____

BIBLICAL EVIDENCE OF
THE SINNER'S SEPARATION FROM GOD

Having considered several of the necessary implications of separation from God, we will now look specifically at what the Scriptures teach about this aspect of God's judgment of the sinner.

1. According to Genesis 2:16-17, what would be the penalty if Adam disobeyed God's command? What is the extent of this penalty?

NOTES: The penalty for Adam's sin would be death. This death would be not only physical but also spiritual and relational. Relationally, Adam would be estranged from God and the life that finds its source in Him. All the other maladies that Adam experienced were a direct result of this rupture in fellowship.

2. In Genesis 3:24, the initial separation between God and man is powerfully illustrated. Describe this event, and explain how it applies to all men.

_____

_____

_____

_____

_____

_____

_____

> **NOTES:** The word "drove" is translated from the Hebrew verb **garish**, which means, "to drive out, cast out, or expel." In His holiness, righteousness, and justice, God acted upon man in judgment. At the same time, this was an act of divine mercy to keep man from living forever in his miserable, fallen state: "Then the Lord God said, 'Behold, the man has become like one of Us in knowing good and evil. Now, lest he stretch out his hand and take also of the tree of life and eat, and live forever'" (Genesis 3:22).

3. In His holiness, God cannot be neutral toward sin or toward those who practice it; rather, He must hate sin and turn away from it as an abomination. What does Habakkuk 1:13 teach us about this truth?

_____

_____

_____

_____

_____

4. The Scriptures teach us not only that sin is repugnant to God, but also that it results in broken fellowship between God and the sinner. What do the following Scriptures teach about this truth?

a. *Proverbs 15:29*

_____

_____

_____

_____

_____

b. *Isaiah 59:1-2*

_____

_____

_____

_____

_____

NOTES: The separation between God and the sinner is not the result of some moral flaw in God's character or a lack in His power. This separation is the direct result of man's shortcomings—his moral corruption and his obstinate sin.

5. In the book of Ephesians, we find several texts that describe the great separation that existed between the pagan Gentiles and the one true God. These passages also serve well to illustrate the great separation that exists between God and any sinner, Jew or Gentile. How are sinners described in the following Scriptures?

a. S_____ *from Christ (2:12).*

b. A_____ from the commonwealth of Israel (2:12). From the Greek verb **apallotrióō**, this word can also be translated, "to exclude" or "to estrange." The word "commonwealth" may also be translated, "citizenship" (NET).

c. S_____ to the covenants of promise (2:12). This comes from the Greek word **xénos**, which can also be translated, "foreigner."

d. Having no H_____ (2:12).

e. Without G_____ in the world (2:12). Man has no hope apart from the God of the Scriptures and the promise of reconciliation and eternal life through the atoning work of Jesus Christ.

f. S_____ and A_____ (2:19). The word "strangers" comes from the Greek word **xénos**, which can also be translated "foreigner." The word "aliens" comes from the Greek word **pároikos**, [**pará** = by the side of + **oíkos** = house]; it refers to someone from the outside—a stranger.

g. A_____ from the life of God (4:18). From the Greek verb **apallotrióō**, this word can also be translated, "to exclude" or "to estrange."

6. Psalm 1:6 is a powerful text that helps us understand what it means to be estranged from God. Write your thoughts on this verse.

_____

_____

_____

_____

_____

_____

_____

NOTES: The word "knows" comes from Hebrew word **yada**, which denotes intimate knowledge, relationship, fellowship, and communion. God is intimately acquainted with the righteous and is working in his life for good (Romans 8:28), but He is estranged from the wicked. This does not mean that God's knowledge is limited with regard to those who are wicked or that He does not know their deeds. To the contrary, God knows the most intimate thoughts and hidden deeds of even the most estranged and evil men on earth.

7. Based upon the Scriptures we have studied in Main Points 1-6, explain how man's sin results in broken fellowship and separation from God.

_____

_____

_____

_____

_____

_____

_____

_____

DISCERNING THE PLIGHT OF  MAN

Chapter 18: Exposed to Misery

In the previous chapter, we considered separation from God as one of His judgments of the wicked. We will now consider His judgment in the misery which results from this separation.

Excepting the reality of death, the miseries of this present life are possibly the greatest evidence of God's judgment upon sin. We not only are fallen creatures, but we also live in a fallen world. Even in the fleetingness of our existence, we are encumbered with great difficulties and hardships from without and within.

There is a tendency in our present age of Christianity to explain away these miseries of life as "natural" consequences of sin and deny any possibility that they might be the result of God's sovereignty, justice, and wrath. Many seek to remove any responsibility from God and try to somehow protect Him from accusations of lovelessness or cruelty. Nevertheless, the Scriptures clearly reveal that the temporal miseries of this life are indeed, to varying degrees, a result of God's judgment upon the sinner and the fallen world in which he dwells. Romans 1:18 teaches us that "the wrath of God is **revealed** from heaven against all ungodliness and unrighteousness of men" (emphasis added). The temporal miseries of this world are one aspect of this revelation.

Although the temporal miseries that engulf every aspect of human life are primarily a revelation of God's justice and wrath, they are not devoid of mercy. Every misery and hardship from birth to death is a divine reminder to man of his fallenness, the corruption of his soul, and his alienation from God. The pain of childbirth calls out to man; the calamities, natural disasters, wars, pestilences, and famines of this world call out to man; the disappointments and frustrations of this life call out to man; the inward struggles of dissatisfaction and restlessness call out to man; the ever-present threat of death calls out to man:

> You are lost and must be found. You are alienated and must be reconciled. You are fallen and must be raised. You are dislocated and must be set right. You are disfigured and must be transformed.

1. In Genesis 3:16-19 is found a description of the misery that fell upon mankind and creation as a result of sin. Explain how each misery is a revelation both of God's judgment and of His mercy.

    a. *The Judgment upon the Woman (v.16)*

    _____

    _____

    _____

    _____

_____

_____

_____

> **NOTES:** The clause, "your desire shall be contrary to husband," is literally, "toward your husband will be your desire." It may denote the following: (1) the woman's relationship with her husband would be marked by longing and a lack of fulfillment; (2) the woman, who sought independence from God, would now have an inordinate desire or craving for man; and (3) the relationship between man and woman would be marked by conflict—the woman would "desire" to dominate her husband, and her husband would abuse his authority over her.

b. *The Judgment upon the Man (vv.17-19)*

_____

_____

_____

_____

_____

_____

_____

> **NOTES:** The judgment that fell upon the man can be summed up in three words: toil, futility, and death. This has been the plight of man in every generation. Even the most powerful and wealthiest of men have been unable to escape this judgment. Regardless of prior exploits, every one of them has laid down his head in death and lost all that he had gained.

2. The consequences of the curse that have fallen upon man since the first rebellion of Adam are clearly set before us in the "wisdom literature" of the Scriptures (*i.e.* Job, Psalms, Proverbs, Ecclesiastes, and Song of Solomon). What do the following wisdom literature texts teach us about the inevitable miseries and frustrations of fallen man? How should these truths lead man back to God?

a. *Job 5:7*

_____

_____

_____

_____

_____

_____

NOTES: The meaning of this verse is that trouble and afflictions are as certain and fre-quent for a man as it is certain that sparks will fly upward from an open fire. It is never shocking to see sparks fly upward, because that is what they most commonly do. Simi-larly, it should never be shocking when we see man afflicted with trouble.

b. *Job 7:1-2*

_____

_____

_____

_____

c. *Psalm 89:47*

_____

_____

_____

_____

d. *Ecclesiastes 2:22-23*

Chapter 19: Given Over to Sin

The Scriptures teach that all men are born spiritually dead, morally depraved, and capable of almost limitless evil. If they were allowed to give full rein to their depravity, the result would be the utter elimination of man. For the preservation of society and for His own purpose and glory, God restrains the wickedness of men and keeps them from being as bad as they could be. This restraining work of God is the only thing that stands between humanity and self-annihilation. It is one of the greatest manifestations of God's grace toward all.

The divine act of "giving men over" to their sin occurs when God ceases to restrain man's evil or at least allows man more freedom to exercise his depravity. God withdraws His restraining grace and turns men over to the moral corruption and depravity of their own hearts. This inevitably leads to destruction and is one of the most terrible manifestations of the wrath of God. In this chapter, we will heavily consider one of the darkest texts in the Word of God: Romans 1:18-32. The most terrifying thing about this passage is that the judgment of which it speaks has been manifested in differing degrees in every generation since the fall, including our own. Read Romans 1:18-32 several times until you are familiar with its contents, and then answer the following questions.

1. According to verse 18, against whom is the wrath of God revealed? Why is this so?

_____

_____

_____

_____

_____

NOTES: The word "suppress" comes from the Greek word **katéchō**, which may also be translated, "to restrain, hinder, detain, or hold back."

2. According to verses 19-20, how is it that the Scriptures can rightly declare that all men are "without excuse," even those who have never had the privilege of access to the written revelation of God in the Scriptures?

_____

_____

_____

_____

_____

NOTES: This does not mean that all men know everything that may be known about God or that all men are granted the same degree of revelation. It does mean that all men—everywhere and at all times—possess sufficient knowledge of the one true God so that they will be without excuse for their sins on the Day of Judgment. Though limited, God's revelation of Himself to all men has not been ambiguous or unclear. He has made it "evident" to all men that there is one true God and that He alone should be worshiped. The phrase "within them" proves that the knowledge of the one true God is not demonstrated just through the works of creation; God Himself has imprinted this knowledge upon the very heart of every man. The universe, which God has made and which proves His existence, simply acts as a confirmation or reminder of what all men already know—there is one true God who is worthy of worship and obedience.

3. According to verses 21-25, what has been the universal response of mankind to the revelation of God? How do the following portions describe man's reaction? How has this been evidenced throughout history?

   a. *For although they knew God, they did not honor Him as God or give thanks to Him (v.21).*

   _____

   _____

   _____

   _____

   _____

   b. *But they became futile in their thinking, and their foolish hearts were darkened (v.21).*

   _____

   _____

   _____

_____

_____

NOTES: Man has turned from the light of the omniscient God and constructed his own view of reality. This rebellion has led to intellectual absurdities, moral darkness, and futility.

c. *Claiming to be wise, they became fools (v.22).*

_____

_____

_____

_____

_____

NOTES: When a finite and error-prone mankind sets its knowledge and understanding above that of the omniscient God, the result is the multiplication of fools and foolishness.

d. *And exchanged the glory of the immortal God for images resembling mortal man and birds and animals and creeping things (v.23).*

_____

_____

_____

_____

_____

NOTES: The madness of unbelieving men is most revealed in the objects of their worship. Their self-worship degrades into the worship of even the lowliest creatures.

e. *They exchanged the truth about God for a lie and worshiped and served the creature rather than the Creator, who is blessed forever (v.25).*

_____

_____

_____

_____

_____

> **NOTES:** Throughout history, we see men rejecting the Creator, who is above them, and instead worshiping creatures that are below them.

4. In verse 18, we learned that the wrath of God is revealed from heaven against men who willingly deny and suppress the truth. According to the following verses, **how** has the wrath of God been manifested against them?

   a. *God gave them up in the L_____ of their hearts to I_____ (v.24).* God gave them over to the power of the lusts of their own morally corrupt hearts, and the result is shameful impurity. The word "impurity" comes from the Greek word **akatharsía**, which may also be translated, "uncleanness."

   b. *God gave them up to D_____ passions (v.26).* From the Greek word **atimía**, this word may also be translated, "degrading," "disgraceful," or "shameful." The phrase can be translated literally as "passions of disgrace."

   c. *God gave them up to a D_____ mind (v.28).* From the Greek word **adókimos** [a = negative particle + **dókimos** = tested, approved], the word can also be translated, "rejected," "unqualified," "unapproved," or "worthless." A debased mind is one that cannot stand the test of God's righteousness.

5. According to verses 28-32, what is the ultimate result of God giving men over to be governed by their own hearts?

_____

_____

_____

_____

_____

_____

_____

_____

NOTES: It is important to understand that these vices are not so much the *reason* for God's coming judgment upon mankind as they are the *result* of God having already judged mankind. The greatest sin of mankind is not found among these vices, but in verse 21: "For although they knew God, they did not honor Him as God or give thanks to Him." Because mankind has rejected God and refused to live under His government, God as judged them by turning them over to be governed by their morally corrupt hearts and radically depraved minds. This results in a society filled with the vices that are listed in verses 28-32.

Chapter 20: Death

Part One: A Biblical Description of Death

Without doubt, the greatest proof of the wrath of God against the unrighteousness of man is physical death—the separation of the soul from the body. Beginning with Adam and continuing even now, all men are faced with the terrible and undeniable reality that they will die. Regardless of human greatness, power, or social position, death is the unavoidable destiny that awaits all men. The Scriptures teach us that this terrifying reality is a direct consequence of sin. It is important to note that man's death is not his annihilation. Once dead, men do not cease to be; rather, they continue to exist, either in eternal communion with God in heaven or in eternal separation from Him in hell.

Again, it is necessary that one find in death **both divine judgment and mercy**. Death is "God's great reminder" to man of his mortality and his great need for redemption. Every obituary, every funeral procession, every grave marker cries out to man to turn from the concerns of this world to the concerns of eternity, to make ready for the reaper, and to prepare to meet his God.

Although death is an undeniable reality that confronts mankind relentlessly, its exact nature remains a mystery to the living. We cannot rely upon even the most sincere accounts of those who have supposedly "gone to the other side" and returned to tell others about their experience. If we are to have a "sure word" about so great a mystery, we must turn to the Scriptures.

The Bible speaks often about death, with many warnings and exhortations; yet it offers few answers with regard to its exact nature. What can be known for sure must be gleaned from the few direct references found in the Scriptures. These texts teach us two great truths. **First**, death is not the end of conscious human existence. **Second**, at death, man's body returns to the ground (until the resurrection), and his spirit returns to God.

1. In James 2:26 is found a simple yet profound description of death. Identify the truth taught in this text, and then write your thoughts. What is death? When does death occur?

    a. *The B_____ apart from the S_____ is dead.*

    _____

    _____

    _____

    _____

    _____

2. We can see from James 2:26 that a man's spirit is separated from his body at death. According to Ecclesiastes 12:7 and Psalm 146:4, what happens to the body and the spirit at the moment of separation?

_____

_____

_____

_____

_____

_____

_____

NOTES: It is helpful at this point to remember and consider two important biblical events: (1) the creation of Adam in Genesis 2:7—"Then the Lord God formed the man of dust from the ground and breathed into his nostrils the breath of life, and the man became a living creature"—and (2) the divine curse upon Adam as a result of the fall in Genesis 3:19—"By the sweat of your face you shall eat bread, till you return to the ground, for out of it you were taken; for you are dust, and to dust you shall return."

3. In the Scriptures, several important metaphors are employed to help us understand the nature of death. Identify each of the following metaphors for dying.

a. To B_____ one's L_____ (Genesis 49:33).

b. To P_____ away (Job 34:20).

c. To R_____ to D_____ (Genesis 3:19; Psalm 104:29).

d. To be C_____ off (Job 24:24).

e. To D_____ (II Timothy 4:6; II Peter 1:15).

DISCERNING THE PLIGHT OF MAN

Chapter 21: Death

Part Two: Death as Divine Judgment

DEATH AS A MANIFESTATION OF GOD'S JUDGMENT

From its first mention in the Scriptures, death is treated as the result of God's judgment against the sin of man. Why do humans die? The Bible's response is clear and unapologetic: they die because they are sinners. God declared to Adam, "For in the day that you eat of it [*i.e.* the tree of the knowledge of good and evil] you shall surely die" (Genesis 2:17). From this text and others, it is clear that death was not woven into the fabric of creation from the beginning; rather, it entered into our world through the sin of Adam and has passed on to all men, for all men sin (Romans 5:12). Every tombstone and grave marker is a manifestation of God's judgment against our fallen race. To say that death is always a manifestation of God's judgment does not necessarily mean that some die sooner than others because they are greater sinners. After all, there are children who die in the womb without committing a single act of sin, and there are men who live in open rebellion against God for decades. Therefore, to describe death as a manifestation of God's judgment is simply to say that every one of us is part of a fallen, sinful race and that death is one manifestation of God's judgment against all of us.

1. Throughout the Scriptures, death is seen as the result of man's sin. Whether it is the imputed sin of Adam or the personal unrighteousness of all men, the principle is the same—all men die because all men sin. What do the following Scriptures from the Old and New Testaments teach us about this truth?

   a. *Ezekiel 18:4, 20*

   _____

   _____

   _____

   _____

   _____

   b. *Romans 6:23*

   _____

   _____

_____

_____

_____

> **NOTES:** The word "wages" comes from the Greek word **opsônion**, which may also be translated, "pay," "provision," or "allowance." The term was used of a stipend or the subsistence payment of soldiers.

2. Both the Old and New Testaments are clear and unapologetic: the inevitable consequence of sin is death. In James 1:15, the Scriptures reveal to us the inner workings and the fatal results of sin in the life of man. Read the text several times until you are familiar with its contents, and then write your thoughts.

_____

_____

_____

_____

_____

> **NOTES:** The word "desire" comes from the Greek word **epithumía**, which refers to an intense desire or longing. The term can be either positive or negative, depending on the context. In this verse, it refers to lust or an intense desire that is contrary to the will of God. When lust is allowed to grow or mature, it gives birth to sin. When sin becomes an accomplished act, it brings forth death. The end of sin is always death.

3. In Isaiah 64:6, the relationship between man's sin and death is powerfully illustrated. Read the text until you are familiar with its contents, and then write your thoughts regarding the following questions.

   a. _How is man's moral corruption described?_

   _____

   _____

   _____

_____

_____

NOTES: The word "unclean" is possibly a reference to leprosy (Leviticus 13:8, 45). The comparison of righteous deeds to filthy rags proves that the sinner's inward moral corruption contaminates or pollutes even his most righteous deeds. In the New Testament, Jude 23 describes the sinner's garments as "stained by the flesh."

b. *What are the inevitable consequences of man's moral corruption and active pursuit of sin?*

_____

_____

_____

_____

_____

NOTES: The picture of dry and lifeless leaves being carried away by the winter's wind is a poignant reminder of man's mortality and the futility of his life apart from God.

4. In Psalm 90:2-10 is found a powerful and poetic portrayal of death as a manifestation of God's judgment against sinful men. Write your thoughts on each of the following portions.

a. *You return man to dust and say, "Return, O children of man!" (v.3).*

_____

_____

_____

_____

NOTES: The text is reminiscent of the curse that God declared against Adam after the fall: "By the sweat of your face you shall eat bread, till you return to the ground, for out of it you were taken; for you are dust, and to dust you shall return" (Genesis 3:19).

b. *You sweep them away as with a flood; they are like a dream, like grass that is renewed in the morning: in the morning it flourishes and is renewed; in the evening it fades and withers (vv.5-6).*

_____

_____

_____

_____

_____

NOTES: A similar passage is found in Psalm 103:15-16: "As for man, his days are like grass; he flourishes like a flower of the field; for the wind passes over it, and it is gone, and its place knows it no more."

c. *For we are brought to an end by Your anger; by Your wrath we are dismayed. You have set our iniquities before You, our secret sins in the light of your presence. For all our days pass away under Your wrath; we bring our years to an end like a sigh (vv.7-9).*

_____

_____

_____

_____

_____

NOTES: The psalmist asked, "If You, O Lord, should mark iniquities, O Lord, who could stand?" (Psalm 130:3). This is a rhetorical question with an obvious answer: "No one!"

d. *The years of our life are seventy, or even by reason of strength eighty; yet their span is but toil and trouble; they are soon gone, and we fly away (v.10).*

_____

_____

_____

_____

_____

> **NOTES:** The chain of logic is evident: sin leads to death, and death results in futility. Because of sin, man's life is little more than vanity. Death swallows up whatever glory that man might gain and destroys all hope. The most noble of all of God's earthly creatures is condemned to suffer the anguish of his mortality and the dread of judgment. Only in Jesus Christ is this terrible course reversed!

DEATH AS A SOVEREIGN WORK OF GOD

According to the Scriptures, death is a consequence of God's judgment against man's sin. All men die, and they die according to the sovereign decree of God. He has not only appointed the day of our death, but He Himself will also bring it about. He gives life and takes it; He makes alive and kills. Many within contemporary Christian circles would be extremely hesitant to admit that death is the result of the sovereign decree and work of God. They would instead explain death as a mere consequence of living in a fallen world or as something beyond the control of a loving Creator. This is a blatant contradiction of the testimony of Scripture.

1. How is God described in Daniel 5:23? Complete the description, and then explain its meaning.

    a. *The God in whose H_____ is your B_____, and whose are all your ways.*

    _____

    _____

    _____

    _____

2. The Scriptures are clear and unapologetic that God is absolutely sovereign over the life and death of every man. Below are two of the most important texts in Scripture with regard to this truth. What do they teach us?

    a. *Deuteronomy 32:39*

    _____

    _____

_____

_____

_____

b. *I Samuel 2:6*

_____

_____

_____

_____

NOTES: The word *sheol* is a transliteration from the Hebrew. It most commonly refers to the grave or the place of the dead.

3. The doctrine of God's sovereignty teaches us that the death of every man has already been appointed by divine decree. A certain number of days have been given to each of us. They cannot be extended even one breath beyond what God has determined. What do the following Scriptures teach us about this truth?

a. *Job 14:5*

_____

_____

_____

_____

b. *Ecclesiastes 3:1-2*

_____

_____

c. *Hebrews 9:27*

_____

_____

_____

_____

NOTES: The word "appointed" comes from the Greek word **apókeimai**, which means, "to be laid away, to be laid up in store, or to be reserved." The time of each man's death is subject to God's sovereign decree. It is not ultimately the result of the will of man, random chance, or consequence.

d. *Luke 12:20*

_____

_____

_____

_____

NOTES: Here we see a powerful illustration of Hebrews 9:27. The word "required" is translated from the Greek word **apaíteō**, which means, "to ask or demand back." When God beckons man to come, it is a request he is unable to deny.

Chapter 22: Death

Part Three: Death's Power over Man

THE UNIVERSALITY OF DEATH

One biblical truth that stands without any opponent in any realm (science, history, etc.) is that all men die. The great mass of humanity lives under an unrelenting mortal plague. Billions have fallen from it scourge, and thousands more join their number every day. There is no cure, and there is no hope that this reality will somehow dissipate with time.

Death is so frequent and widespread that it may seem unnecessary to consider its universality. However, it is still important to consider such a doctrine, not because it is denied, but because it is often forgotten or overlooked. We know that we are mortal creatures. We know that we are dying. We know that we cannot escape death or impede its coming. Therefore, we (whether consciously or unconsciously) tend to seek to drive the thought of death as far from us as possible. We have become so proficient at banishing death from our thoughts that we can even carry the caskets of our closest friends without one moment's meditation on the truth that the same fate awaits us all. For this reason, it is necessary for us to hear the very truth we seek to suppress.

1. In the Old Testament, there is a very important metaphor used to communicate the universality of death. Identify this metaphor, and explain its meaning.

    a. *The W_____ of all the E_____ (Joshua 23:14; I Kings 2:1-2).*

    _____

    _____

    _____

    _____

2. An important truth that is often taught in the Scriptures is that death is not a respecter of persons. It comes upon all men alike—rich and poor, wise and foolish. What do the following Scriptures teach us about this truth?

    a. *Job 21:22-26*

    _____

    _____

_____

_____

_____

_____

_____

b. *Ecclesiastes 2:16*

_____

_____

_____

_____

_____

_____

_____

THE BREVITY, FRAILTY, AND FUTILITY OF MAN

The first man was created in the image of God. But so much was lost with the advent of sin; man's existence became tragically twisted and deformed beyond recognition. Man became a being of brief duration, of weariness, and of futility. Now he lives his life until all vitality is drained away, every purpose is demolished, and the body finally returns to the dust from which it came. It is not without reason that the preacher cries out, "Vanity of vanities! All is vanity" (Ecclesiastes 1:2).

1. Throughout the Scriptures are found numerous descriptions of the frailty of man, the brevity of his life, and the futility of all his strivings. In the following are some of the most important texts regarding this theme. Meditate upon each text, and then write your thoughts. What metaphors and similes are used to describe man and his life? What do they communicate?

    a. *Job 14:1-2*

    _____

    _____

_____

_____

b. *Psalm 39:4-6*

_____

_____

_____

_____

c. *Psalm 78:39*

_____

_____

_____

_____

d. *Psalm 103:14-16*

_____

_____

_____

_____

e. *Psalm 144:3-4*

_____

_____

_____

_____

f. *James 4:14*

_____

_____

_____

_____

2. In the book of Job are found two passages that are beneficial in illustrating the frailty and the brevity of man's life. Meditate carefully upon each text, and then write your thoughts.

a. *The Frailty of Man's Life (Job 4:17-21)*

_____

_____

_____

_____

_____

b. *The Brevity of Man's Life (Job 9:25-26)*

_____

_____

_____

_____

_____

3. In the following Scriptures are found a few of the most striking descriptions of the futility and vanity of man's life. Read the texts until you are familiar with their contents, and then write your thoughts. How is the futility of man's life described?

a. *Psalm 49:10-14*

_____

_____

_____

_____

b. *Ecclesiastes 3:19-20*

_____

_____

_____

NOTES: It is important to note that this is not a denial of the immortality of the human soul or of the future resurrection of the righteous and the unrighteous. The writer is making a declaration with regard to reality as it appears to the physical senses. His main point is only that all men die.

c. *Ecclesiastes 5:15-17*

_____

_____

_____

d. *I Timothy 6:7*

_____

_____

_____

_____

4. The Scriptures teach that all men sin and that, because of this, all men die. Death is the inevitable reality that awaits every one of us. It is our unavoidable, inescapable, and undefeatable enemy. What do the following passages of Scriptures teach us about this truth?

   a. *Job 14:7-12*

   _____

   _____

   _____

   _____

   b. *Psalm 49:7-9*

   _____

   _____

   _____

   _____

   c. *Psalm 89:47-48*

   _____

   _____

   _____

   _____

   d. *Ecclesiastes 8:8*

   _____

_____

_____

5. To bring our study of the frailty of man and the brevity of his life to a close we will consider two final texts of Scripture: Isaiah 40:6-8 and Ecclesiastes 12:1. In the former is found one of the most powerful declarations regarding both the brevity of man and the eternity of God. In the latter is found an extremely important admonition to all men. Read each text until you are familiar with its contents, and then write the truths that you have gleaned.

a. *The Truth About Man (Isaiah 40:6-8)*

_____

_____

_____

_____

_____

b. *How Then Shall We Live? (Ecclesiastes 12:1)*

_____

_____

_____

_____

_____

Chapter 23: The Final Judgment of the Wicked

Possibly the most awesome doctrine in all the Scriptures is that of the final judgment. This doctrine—that every one of Adam's race will stand before a righteous and all-knowing God and be judged according to his or her every thought, word, and deed—is something that goes beyond the scope of our wildest imaginations.

Although the doctrine of the final judgment is often scorned and rejected as a relic from the past, it must be remembered that it is the clear teaching of Scripture and a reasonable truth to accept in light of what we know about the attributes of God. It is certainly God's prerogative both to govern the creatures He has created and to judge the creatures He governs. In fact, it is not just His prerogative, but it is demanded by His righteous character. Shall not the Judge of all the earth do right (Genesis 18:25)? Is it not indeed **necessary** that a moral God carry out moral justice in the universe that He has made? Shall we deny God the very right we demand for ourselves in our own courts of law? Certainly not!

The final judgment is a **fundamental doctrine of the Scriptures**. It is impossible to hold to the divine inspiration and infallibility of the Bible without embracing the doctrine of the final judgment and eternal condemnation of the wicked. Although much about this doctrine remains a mystery, it nevertheless is an absolute certainty according to the Scriptures. Each and every one of Adam's race will be judged by God. The wicked will be condemned to eternal punishment, and the redeemed in Christ will inherit the fullness of salvation.

1. The final judgment is an essential doctrine of the Scriptures and the Christian faith. This truth is clearly communicated in Hebrews 6:1-2. How does the writer refer to the doctrine?

    a. *An E_____ doctrine about the Christ.*

    > **NOTES:** The word comes from the Greek word **archê**, which denotes a beginning or origin. The phrase "elementary doctrine" means literally, "word of the beginning." It tells us that the doctrine of eternal judgment is a beginning or foundational teaching of Christianity. It is not a theological speculation; it is a biblical certainty.

2. God's final judgment of mankind is so embedded in Old Testament thought that to deny its reality would be to deny the infallibility of the Scriptures. What do the following Old Testament passages teach us about the certainty of God's final judgment?

    a. *Psalm 9:7-8*

    _____

    _____

b. *Psalm 96:10-13*

c. *Ecclesiastes 3:17*

d. *Ecclesiastes 11:9*

e. *Ecclesiastes 12:13-14*

3. It is important to understand that the truth of the final judgment is not merely an "Old Testament doctrine." What do the following New Testament texts teach us about the certainty of God's final judgment?

    a. *Romans 14:10-12*

    _____

    _____

    _____

    _____

    b. *Hebrews 9:27*

    _____

    _____

    _____

    _____

    c. *II Peter 3:7*

    _____

    _____

    _____

    _____

4. In the Scriptures, there are many names given to describe the day when God will judge all men. Identify each name according to the Scripture given, and then write your thoughts on what each name communicates to us.

    a. *The D_____ of J_____ (II Peter 2:9).*

    _____

    _____

_____

_____

_____

NOTES: The word "judgment" comes from the Greek word **krísis**, from which the English word "crisis" is derived. It denotes a legal judgment or a judicial decision or evaluation. The phrase here indicates the day when the omniscient God evaluates and decides the fate of all men. His decision will never be overturned.

b. *The day of W_____ when God's R_____ judgment will be revealed (Romans 2:5).*

_____

_____

_____

_____

NOTES: On the Day of Judgment, God's perfect righteousness will be revealed. Every man will be given exactly what he deserves, whether reward or wrath. On that day, no one will doubt that God is righteous.

c. *The G_____ day (Jude 6).*

_____

_____

_____

_____

NOTES: The word "great" comes from the Greek word **mégas**. If the greatness of a day is determined by its relevance and significance for humanity, the Day of Judgment stands out above all the rest. On that day, the eternal fate of all men will be decided.

d. The D_____ of G_____ (II Peter 3:12).

_____

_____

_____

_____

NOTES: The Day of Judgment will be God's day. It will be a day when God will be vindicated before all creation. All doubts with regard to His existence and character will be put away.

5. On the Day of Judgment, God will consider the thoughts, words, and deeds of every member of Adam's race. What do the following Scriptures teach us about the thoroughness of God's judgment? Will anything be overlooked or hidden before Him?

a. Mark 4:22; Luke 8:17; 12:2-3

_____

_____

_____

_____

b. Ecclesiastes 12:14

_____

_____

_____

_____

c. *I Corinthians 4:5*

_____

_____

_____

_____

_____

d. *Hebrews 4:13*

_____

_____

_____

_____

_____

NOTES: The word "naked" is a literal translation of the Greek word ***gumnós***. The word "exposed" comes from the Greek word ***trachēlízō***, which means, "to lay bare the neck." It is used outside the New Testament to describe the pulling back of a sacrificial victim's neck in order to expose it for slaughter.

6. In Revelation 20:11-15 is found the most descriptive passage in the Scriptures regarding the final judgment. Read the text several times until you are familiar with its contents, and then answer the following questions.

a. *How are God and the throne of God described in verse 11? How are the greatness and holiness of God communicated?*

_____

_____

_____

_____

_____

_____

NOTES: The throne demonstrates God's absolute sovereignty over all creation. The whiteness of the throne signifies the holiness or moral purity of the One who sits upon it.

b. *According to verses 12-13, who are standing before the throne of God? Does anyone escape from the judgment? Is anyone exempt? Explain your answer.*

_____

_____

_____

_____

_____

c. *According to verses 12-13, how are men judged? What is the basis for God's judgment? Is the judgment thorough? Explain your answer.*

_____

_____

_____

_____

_____

NOTES: The plurality of the word "books" indicates the completeness and extensiveness of God's record of every man's deeds. The repetition of the phrase, "according to what they had done," seeks to drive home to the reader the fact that all men will be judged according to their every thought, word, and deed. For the thinking man, this truth is terrifying!

d. *According to verses 14-15, what is the fate of every person who rejects Jesus Christ and is judged according his own deeds?*

_____

_____

_____

_____

_____

NOTES: This is the terrifying reality that cannot be explained away. It is the great and certain truth of the Scriptures that unending punishment awaits all those who have rejected God's mercy. In the following chapters, we will consider this biblical doctrine of everlasting punishment.

Chapter 24: Hell

Part One: The Nature of Hell

We have learned that the wrath of God is manifested in man's alienation from God—his being turned over to sin, exposed to misery, and subjected to physical death. In the following, we will consider the greatest of all manifestations of divine wrath: **hell**. One of the most solemn truths of Scripture is that the consequences of sin do not end with physical death. After death, there is a final judgment, and those who die in their sins are sentenced to spend eternity in hell. Even though this doctrine is often ridiculed and rejected, we cannot ignore the clear teaching of Scripture. There is a place of eternal judgment for the wicked.

In any attempt to understand the nature of hell, we must proceed with much caution. On the one hand, we must be careful to follow the Scriptures and not the fanciful descriptions of hell created by both ancient and modern literature and media. On the other hand, we must be careful not to explain away the doctrine of hell or diminish its horrors. According to the Scriptures, and especially the teachings of Jesus Christ, there is a real place called "hell" that is both terrible in its suffering and eternal in it duration.

HADES AND GEHENNA

In the New Testament, two specific terms are used with reference to hell: **Hades** and **Gehenna**. We can come to a clearer understanding of the nature of hell through a careful study of these two references.

HADES

The word "Hades" comes from the Greek word **hádēs**, which occurs ten times in the New Testament.[6] Although it is most often employed as a reference to death and the general abode of the dead, it is clearly used in Luke 16:23 with reference to a place where the wicked are tormented. There are two major interpretations with regard to Hades and its relationship to Gehenna: either (1) Hades is the temporary abode of the wicked until the last judgment when the wicked are reunited with their resurrected bodies and assigned to an eternal place of torment known as Gehenna; or (2) Hades and Gehenna are both references to the same place of torment. In the latter interpretation, the wicked suffer in a disembodied state before the last judgment and the resurrection. Then, after the resurrection and the last judgment, the wicked are united with their resurrected bodies and returned to the same place of torment.

GEHENNA

The word "Gehenna" (translated as "hell" in the Scriptures) is the Latin form of the Aramaic expression **gehinnam**; it refers to the **valley of Hinnom** (see Joshua 15:8), which is located south of Jerusalem (today it is known as **Wadi er-Rababi**). The Greek form of this word is **géenna**,

---

[6] Matthew 11:23; 16:18; Luke 10:15; 16:23; Acts 2:27, 31; Revelation 1:18; 6:8; 20:13, 14

which occurs twelve times in the New Testament.[7] Under the reigns of the wicked kings Ahaz and Manasseh, it was a place where parents offered their children as sacrifices to the Ammonite god Molech (Jeremiah 32:35; see also II Kings 16:3; 21:6). During the reign of Josiah, the practice of child sacrifice was ended, and the valley of Hinnom was desecrated (II Kings 23:10-14). It eventually became a refuse pile for garbage, the carcasses of dead animals, and the bodies of executed criminals. It was a place of continuous fire and smoke and was infested with maggots, worms, and vermin. By the time of Christ, the word was commonly employed to denote the place of final punishment and torment for the wicked—a place of eternal death, pollution, defilement, and misery.

EXCLUSION FROM THE FAVORABLE PRESENCE OF GOD

Possibly the most terrible truth about hell is that it is exclusion from the favorable presence of God. In modern Evangelical thinking, hell is often described as a place of torment outside of God's presence. It is often said that heaven is heaven because God is there, while hell is hell because God is not there. Although this statement contains an element of truth, it is extremely misleading. It is not the absence of God that makes hell a place of torment, but the absence of **His favorable presence**. In fact, hell is hell because God **is** there in the fullness of His justice and wrath.

1. II Thessalonians 1:9 is one of the most important texts in the Scriptures with regard to the separation of the wicked from the favorable presence of God. Read the text until you are familiar with its contents, and then write your thoughts.

_____

_____

_____

_____

NOTES: The phrase "away from" comes from the Greek preposition **apó**, which has been interpreted and translated in two different ways: (1) "away from the presence of the Lord," meaning that the punishment itself exists in being separated from the Lord; or (2) "from the presence of the Lord," meaning that the punishment comes forth from the Lord's presence. Either way, the phrase, "from the presence of the Lord," cannot mean that nothing of God's presence or power exists in hell, as hell is itself a manifestation of His wrath.

2. In the Scriptures, several texts refer to man's final judgment and sentence to hell as his being cast out or excluded from the favorable presence of God. Consider each text carefully, and then write your thoughts.

---

[7] Matthew 5:22, 29, 30; 10:28; 18:9; 23:15, 33; Mark 9:43, 45, 47; Luke 12:5; James 3:6

a. *Matthew 7:23 (see also Luke 13:27)*

_____

_____

_____

_____

b. *Matthew 25:30 (see also 8:12; 22:13)*

_____

_____

_____

_____

3. It is not the absence of God that makes hell a place of torment, but the absence of His favorable presence. Hell is hell because God is there in the fullness of His justice and wrath. What does Revelation 14:9-10 teach us about this truth?

_____

_____

_____

_____

_____

_____

NOTES: The wicked will not only be judged and sentenced by the Lamb, but their ongoing punishment will also be under His watch. At Christ's coming, the wicked will cry out for the mountains and rocks to fall upon them to hide them from the presence of Him who sits on the throne and from wrath of the Lamb (Luke 23:30; Revelation 6:16). However, their petition will be denied throughout all eternity.

INDESCRIBABLE SUFFERING

It is impossible to be faithful to the Scriptures, especially to the words of Jesus, and at the same time seek to deny or ignore the truths that they teach regarding the suffering of the wicked in hell. As we will see, the Scriptures—especially the Gospels—describe hell as a place of indescribable suffering. It is rightly said that the bliss of heaven goes beyond the power of the mind to comprehend and the power of human language to communicate. According to the Scriptures, the same may be said of the sufferings and terrors of hell. It is important to remember that, although the doctrine of hell is repulsive to many, it is nevertheless most certainly true.

Before we proceed, it is important to understand that hell is not a place where the wicked are cruelly tortured; rather, it is where they suffer **perfect justice** for their sin. God is not cruel. He does not gleefully torture his enemies. In fact, the Bible teaches that God takes no pleasure in the death of the wicked (Ezekiel 18:23, 32). Nevertheless, God is a God of justice, and hell is the place where that justice is dispensed on the wicked. They receive the exact measure of punishment that is due them.

1. In the following Scriptures, how does Jesus describe hell and the suffering therein?

   a. *A place of T_____ (Luke 16:28).* From the Greek word **básanos**, this word refers to severe pain often associated with torture. However, we must remember that hell is not a place of demonic torture as described in Dante's *Inferno*;[8] rather, it is a place of perfect justice, where every man is paid the exact measure of what he deserves.

   b. *A place where there is W_____ and G_____ of teeth (Matthew 8:12).* This description of the sufferings of the wicked in hell is important because of its frequent use by Jesus (Matthew 13:42, 50; 22:13; 24:51; 25:30; Luke 13:28). Hell is a place of pain, anguish, and regret.

2. The following two passages of Scripture reveal to us something of the indescribable suffering in hell. Read through each passage until you are familiar with the contents, and then summarize what is revealed to us about the torments of hell.

   a. *Luke 16:19-31*

   _____

   _____

   _____

   _____

   _____

---

[8] *Inferno* is the first part of fourteenth-century poet Dante Alighieri's epic *Divine Comedy*; it describes the author's allegorical "journey" through several "circles" of hell.

> **NOTES:** Because the story of the rich man and Lazarus has similar characteristics to a parable, some have sought to dismiss this description of hell as merely figurative. However, although it is uncertain how literally we should interpret every detail of the story, there are certain undeniable truths that can be gleaned: (1) after death, there is a separation of the righteous and the wicked; and (2) the righteous are comforted with eternal reward, while the wicked suffer eternal and conscious punishment.

    b. *Revelation 14:9-11*

_____

_____

_____

_____

3. Although the Bible makes it clear that every inhabitant in hell will suffer unspeakable torment, it also teaches that this suffering will be according to the sinfulness of each person's life. What do the following Scriptures teach us about this truth?

    a. *Matthew 11:21-24*

_____

_____

_____

_____

    b. *Luke 12:47-48*

_____

_____

_____

_____

_____

c. *Matthew 23:14; Mark 12:38-40*

_____

_____

_____

_____

_____

NOTES: In Matthew 11:21-24 and Luke 12:47-48, we learn that men are held responsible according to the revelation that has been given to them. In Matthew 23:14 and Mark 12:40, we learn that men will also be judged according to the severity of their sins.

UNENDING PUNISHMENT

Possibly the most frightening truth about hell is that it is everlasting. All who pass through its gates are without any hope of future redemption or restoration. They are forever condemned. This truth is probably the most repulsive one to those who reject the biblical doctrine of hell. How can unending punishment be just? Does not the punishment far exceed the crime?

When thinking about the everlasting nature of hell, two truths must be considered. **First**, we must take into account the abhorrent nature of sin. Sin committed against an infinitely worthy God is deserving of unending punishment. **Second**, we must realize that the punishment of hell is eternal because the wicked continue in their rebellion without repentance throughout eternity. We must not assume that the wicked will repent on the Day of Judgment or even after a short stay in hell. Rather, their hatred of God, hardness of heart, and shameless rebellion will continue throughout eternity! Everlasting rebellion demands everlasting punishment.

1. How is hell described in the following Scriptures? Consider what these descriptions communicate to us about the eternal nature of hell.

   a. E_____ F_____ (*Matthew 18:8; 25:41; Jude 7*).

   b. E_____ P_____ (*Matthew 25:46*). It is important to note that eternal life is mentioned in the same verse as eternal punishment. If we accept the doctrine of the eternal bliss of the righteous in heaven, we must also accept the doctrine of the eternal punishment of the wicked in hell.

c. E_____ D_____ (II Thessalonians 1:9).
Although some would wrongly argue that the word "destruction" indicates a ceasing of existence, the word "eternal" renders this interpretation impossible. In hell, the wicked are given over to an existence that can rightly be described as continuous destruction.

2. What do the following biblical texts teach us about the eternal nature of hell and the eternal punishment measured out upon the wicked?

a. *Matthew 25:41*

_____

_____

_____

_____

_____

b. *Mark 9:47-48*

_____

_____

_____

_____

c. *Revelation 14:9-11*

_____

_____

_____

_____

3. Many who deny the eternal nature of hell would never deny the eternal nature of heaven. However, as mentioned above, consistency requires that if one rejects the eternal nature of hell, he must also reject the eternal nature of heaven. How does Jesus demonstrate this logic? Fill in the blanks.

   a. *According to Matthew 25:46, the wicked go away into E_____*

      punishment, and the righteous go away into E_____ life.

   NOTES: It would be inconsistent to give two conflicting meanings to the same word in the same sentence. If "eternal" punishment does not really mean that the wicked are punished forever, then "eternal" life does not really mean that the righteous live forever in the presence of God.

Chapter 25: Hell

Part Two: The Terrors of Hell

A BIBLICAL DESCRIPTION OF HELL

In the Scriptures, many graphic and striking descriptions of hell are given. Whether they are to be taken as literal or not has been a longstanding debate even among conservative scholars. Is hell a place of literal fire and darkness, of brimstone, and of smoke? If someone denies a literal interpretation of these descriptions in order to hold a view that diminishes the sufferings of the wicked in hell, his arguments are to be dismissed. It is, however, understandable and acceptable to believe these descriptions to be figurative in the sense that they are an attempt to describe something so terrifying that it goes beyond the capacity of the human mind to conceive and beyond the power of human language to communicate. The biblical writers used the greatest terrors known to man on earth to describe the terrors of hell, but we can be assured that the frightfulness of hell is worse than anything found on earth. Fire, darkness, brimstone, and smoke are only feeble attempts to describe a reality far more terrifying than even these words can convey. In the same way that the glories of heaven cannot be comprehended by the human mind or communicated through human language, the terrors of hell are beyond our comprehension and ability to describe.

1. What descriptions do the following Scriptures use to communicate the terrifying nature of hell?

    a. F_____ (Matthew 3:10; 7:19). Throughout the Scriptures, the idea of fire is used to communicate the **judgment** and **wrath** of God revealed against sin and the sinner. It is God's holy and just reaction to all that contradicts His nature and will. It is fierce, terrifying, and irresistible. But as terrifying as literal fire is to a burning man, it cannot begin to describe the terrible fire of God's wrath that is measured out against the wicked in hell.

    b. E_____ F_____ (Matthew 18:8; 25:41). The emphasis here is that the sufferings of the wicked in hell last **forever**. There is no hope of redemption or restoration for those in hell.

    c. U_____ F_____ (Matthew 3:12). The idea communicated here is that the torments of hell will be not only everlasting but also **undiminishing**. There will never any relief for the condemned.

    d. L_____ of F_____ and S_____ (Revelation 20:10). This description is given to communicate the **immensity** and **power** of hell. Hell's judgment is not just a sprinkle or small stream of torment. The inhabitants of hell will be like men shipwrecked in a massive, churning sea of God's wrath, battered and cast to and fro by the violent and neverending waves of God's righteous indignation. They will be as men drowning in a massive, churning cauldron of fire.

154

e. F_____ F_____ (Matthew 13:42). The truth communicated here is of hell's **intensity**. In a furnace, there is little opportunity for the heat to escape, no rain to dampen the flames, and no breeze to bring refreshment or relief. In the same way, the intensity of hell's sufferings will never be reduced.

f. O_____ D_____ (Matthew 8:12; 22:13; 25:30). The truth communicated here is of the **alienation** of hell's inhabitants. They are cast out, and no place is found for them. They are alienated not only from God, but also from fellowship with others. Hell is a place of absolute and unbearable isolation, completely separated from the life and light of God.

g. U_____ D_____ (Jude 13). There are very few things more solitary or more incarcerating than pitch-black darkness. There is the greatest sense of **hopelessness** related to the doom of such darkness.

h. S_____ D_____ (Revelation 20:14; 21:8). The final destiny of the wicked is the very opposite of the believer. There will no longer be a fear of death for the believer (Hebrews 2:14-15), because death will be no more (Revelation 21:4). In contrast, the wicked will live in a state of **unceasing death**. They will have a conscious existence; but they will have none of the blessings, hopes, or joys of life.

2. Having considered some of the descriptive names of hell, write your thoughts. How would you describe hell to another?

_____

_____

_____

_____

_____

_____

_____

_____

WARNINGS TO AVOID HELL AT ANY COST

The terrors of hell are clearly communicated in the warnings of Scripture to avoid hell at any cost. Of all the terrors that could ever come upon a man, hell is the worst. It is important to note that Jesus Christ spoke more about hell than all other biblical persons combined. He clearly and unapologetically taught about the realities of hell and gave men the greatest and gravest warnings to flee from the wrath to come.

1. In Matthew 10:28 and Luke 12:5 are two of the gravest warnings given by Jesus Christ concerning the terrors of hell. Write your thoughts. What do these warnings communicate to us about the terrors of hell and the need to fear it?

_____

_____

_____

_____

_____

NOTES: The world at the time of Jesus was full of war, hostility, mercenaries, and ruthless tyrants. The Roman army could be as cruel as it was powerful. Yet, despite all these dangers that the early church would have to face, Jesus warned His disciples to fear God above them all. The most enduring tortures of this life are limited both in their intensity and in their duration, but the wrath of God in hell is incomprehensible and endless!

2. Jesus and the biblical writers not only taught about the terrors of hell, but they also warned men to avoid the condemnation of hell at any cost. What do the following Scriptures teach us regarding this truth?

   a. *Luke 13:24*

_____

_____

_____

_____

NOTES: The word "strive" comes from a Greek word *agōnízomai*, meaning, "to contend, agonize, and labor fervently or with tremendous zeal."

b. *Matthew 18:8; Mark 9:47*

_____

_____

_____

_____

NOTES: These passages are not to be taken literally—Jesus is not teaching self-mutilation as an effective and proper means of restraining our sinful passions. He is simply teaching that we must deal radically with sin because of its terrifying consequences.

3. Having considered the biblical warning to avoid hell at any cost, write your thoughts. How would you warn another regarding hell?

_____

_____

_____

_____

_____

_____

_____

Chapter 26: Man's Only Hope

THE HOPE OF SALVATION

We have come to the end of our study about man and his plight. We have reached some very solemn conclusions in the course of our study. The sin of Adam has pervaded the entire human race. Every man is a morally corrupt being, hostile toward God and unwilling to submit to His will. All of us are capable of unspeakable sins and perversions and are therefore worthy of the just condemnation of a holy and righteous God. The Scriptures are clear: all men, without exception, stand condemned before God without excuse or alibi. Furthermore, man can do nothing to change his circumstance or to reconcile himself to God. This is a dreadful truth, but it is one that we must believe and accept before we can begin to comprehend the great salvation that God has accomplished for His people through Jesus Christ.

1. The following Scriptures are a fitting conclusion for this study, because they not only declare the solemn truth about our inability to save ourselves, but they also proclaim the great hope of salvation through the mercy of God revealed in Jesus Christ. Consider each Scripture passage; then write out the **solemn truth** and the **great hope** found in each of them.

   a. *Psalm 130:3-4*

   (1) The Solemn Truth (v.3)

   _____

   _____

   _____

   _____

   (2) The Great Hope (v.4)

   _____

   _____

   _____

   _____

b. *Romans 3:19-22*

   (1) The Solemn Truth (vv.19-20)

---

   (2) The Great Hope (vv.21-22)

---

c. *Romans 3:23-26*

   (1) The Solemn Truth (v.23)

---

   (2) The Great Hope (vv.24-26)

---

d. *Romans 7:24-8:2*

(1) The Solemn Truth (7:24)

_____

_____

_____

_____

(2) The Great Hope (7:25-8:2)

_____

_____

_____

_____

e. *Galatians 3:22*

(1) The Solemn Truth

_____

_____

_____

_____

(2) The Great Hope

_____

_____

_____

_____

2. Having considered the both the solemnity and the hopefulness expressed in these passages, write your thoughts. Where does man's only hope lie?

_____

_____

_____

_____

_____

_____

_____

_____

THE PLIGHT OF MAN

The truth about man and his plight is devastating to anyone whose conscience has been awakened by the Holy Spirit. As the Apostle Paul cried out, "Wretched man that I am! Who will deliver me from this body of this death?" (Romans 7:24). The answer to Paul's question and solution to man's dreadful predicament is found in Christ alone—in the gospel (or "good news") of His saving work on our behalf![9]

The Psalmist indicates that if the Lord should keep a record of our trespasses against Him, there would not be a single man on earth who could stand before Him in judgment (Psalm 130:3). Our iniquities have gone over our heads; as a heavy burden, their weight is too much for us to bear (Psalm 38:4). Sin is mankind's greatest problem and the sole source of all the maladies that ruin us as individuals and as collective societies. Therefore, our two greatest needs are salvation from the condemnation of sin and deliverance from its power. Both of these are supplied in the person of Jesus Christ and in His saving work on our behalf.

The Bible declares unequivocally that God is "merciful and gracious, slow to anger, and abounding in steadfast love and faithfulness" (Exodus 34:6). Therefore, He does not take delight in the death of the wicked; rather, He would have him turn from his way and live (Ezekiel 18:23). Regardless of the depth of a man's sin or the extent of his rebellion, he is offered both pardon and cleansing if he will forsake his way and return to the Lord. David even goes so far as to say that God will forgive his lawless deeds, cover his sins, and no longer take his trespasses into account (Psalm 32:1-2).

This is astounding news, but it does present us with something of a theological or philosophical dilemma: how can a good and righteous God grant pardon to wicked men? Shall not the Judge of all the earth do right (Genesis 18:25)? Can a just God be apathetic toward sin or sweep

[9] The doctrine of the gospel and many of the Scriptures that pertain to it are considered in detail in my previous workbook, _Discovering the Glorious Gospel._

it under the rug, so to speak, as though it never happened? Can a holy God bring wicked men into fellowship with Himself and still be holy? The Scriptures themselves declare that he who justifies the wicked is "an abomination to the Lord" (Proverbs 17:15). How then can God forgive the wicked without compromising His own character? Again, the answer is found in the person and work of Christ.

According to the Scriptures, man has sinned (Romans 3:23), and the wages of sin is death (Romans 6:23). God is just, and the demands of His law must be satisfied before the guilty can be pardoned. In the fullness of time, the Son of God became a Man and walked on this earth in perfect obedience to the law of God (Galatians 4:4). At the end of His life and according to the will of the Father, He was crucified by the hands of wicked men (Acts 2:23). On the cross, He stood in the place of His guilty people, and their sin was imputed to Him (II Corinthians 5:21). As the Sin-Bearer, He became accursed of God (Galatians 3:13), forsaken of God (Matthew 27:46), and crushed under the weight of God's wrath (Isaiah 53:10). Through His death, the debt for sin was paid, the demands of God's justice were satisfied, and the wrath of God was appeased. In this manner, God solved the great dilemma. He has justly punished the sins of His people in the death of His only Son; therefore, He may freely justify all who place their hope in Him!

Through the death of His Son, God may now be both just and the justifier of even the most vile sinner who places his faith in Him (Romans 3:26). However, the gospel is more than liberation from the condemnation of sin; it is also deliverance from sin's power. In his first epistle, the Apostle John tells us, "Everyone who believes that Jesus is the Christ has been born of God" (I John 5:1). This new birth both enables a man to repent and believe unto salvation and enables him to walk in newness of life (Romans 6:4). Through the regenerating work of the Holy Spirit, a man's heart of stone, which was spiritually dead and unresponsive to God, is replaced with a heart of living flesh that is both willing and able to hear His voice and follow Him (Ezekiel 36:25-27). He was once a bad tree and bore bad fruit; now he is now a good tree planted by streams of water, yielding fruit in its season with leaves that do not wither (Matthew 7:17-18; Psalm 1:3). Thus the believer is justified, and thus he is the very workmanship of God created in Christ Jesus for good works (Ephesians 2:10). In fact, this ongoing moral transformation in the believer's life is the basis of his assurance and the evidence of true conversion.

As we have said, the gospel is astounding news; but important questions remain: "How may salvation be obtained? What must a man do to be saved?" The answer is clear: he must "repent and believe in the gospel" (Mark 1:15). The many Scriptures in this workbook have already refuted any argument or suggestion that a man might be saved by his own virtue or merit. In ourselves, we are destitute of both! Even our so-called "righteous deeds" before other men are nothing but filthy rags before God (Isaiah 64:6). Therefore, we must reject any and all confidence in the flesh and trust in Christ alone (Philippians 3:3). The Christian is the person who has agreed with God concerning his sinful state, has renounced all confidence in his own virtue and merit, and has placed all his hope for salvation in the person and work of Jesus Christ.

MISSIONARY SOCIETY

HeartCry Missionary Society at a Glance:

The HeartCry Missionary Society began in 1988 in the country of Peru with a desire to aid indigenous or native missionaries so that they might reach their own peoples and establish biblical churches among them. Since then, the Lord has expanded our borders to include not only Latin America but also Africa, Asia, Eurasia, Europe, the Middle East, and North America.

The goal of our ministry is to facilitate the advancement of indigenous missionaries throughout the world. Our strategy consists of four primary components: financial support, theological training, Scripture and literature distribution, and the supply of any tool necessary to facilitate the completion of the Great Commission.

We currently support approximately 250 missionary families (along with a number of ongoing projects) in over 40 nations around the globe.

Introduction to HeartCry

HeartCry Missionary Society was founded and still exists for the advancement of four major goals:

• The Glory of God
• The Benefit of Man
• The Establishment of Biblical Churches
• The Demonstration of God's Faithfulness

1: The Glory of God

Our first major goal is the glory of God. Our greatest concern is that His Name be great among the nations from the rising to the setting of the sun (Malachi 1:11) and that the Lamb who was slain might receive the full reward for His sufferings (Revelation 7:9-10). We find our great purpose and motivation not in man or his needs but in God Himself; in His commitment to His own glory; and in our God-given desire to see Him worshiped in every nation, tribe, people, and language. We find our great confidence not in the Church's ability to fulfill the Great Commission, but in God's unlimited and unhindered power to accomplish all He has decreed.

2. The Benefit of Man

Our second major goal is the salvation of a lost and dying humanity. The Christian who is truly passionate about the glory of God and confident in His sovereignty will not be unmoved by the billions of people in the world who have "had no news" of the gospel of Jesus Christ (Romans 15:21). If we are truly Christ-like, the lost multitude of humanity will move us to compassion (Matthew 9:36), even to great sorrow and unceasing grief (Romans 9:2). The sincerity of our Christian confession should be questioned if we are not willing to do all within our means to make Christ known among the nations and to endure all things for the sake of God's elect (II Timothy 2:10).

3. The Establishment of Local Churches

Our third major goal is the establishment of biblical churches. While we recognize that the needs of mankind are many and his sufferings are diverse, we believe that they all spring from a common origin: the radical depravity of his heart, his enmity toward God, and his rejection of truth. Therefore, we believe that the greatest possible benefit to mankind comes through the preaching of the gospel and the establishment of local churches that proclaim the full counsel of God's Word and minister according to its commands, precepts, and wisdom. Such a work cannot be accomplished through the arm of the flesh, but only through the supernatural providence of God and the means which He has ordained: biblical preaching, intercessory prayer, sacrificial service, unconditional love, and true Christ-likeness.

4. The Demonstration of God's Faithfulness

The fourth and final goal at HeartCry is to demonstrate to God's people that He is truly able and willing to supply all our needs according to His riches in glory. The needs of this ministry will be obtained through prayer. We will not raise support through self-promotion, prodding, or manipulating our brothers and sisters in Christ. If this ministry is of the Lord, then He will be our Patron. If He is with us, He will direct His people to give, and we will prosper. If He is not with us, we will not and should not succeed. Admittedly, our faith has always been meager and frail throughout the years; but God has always been faithful. As one dear brother puts it: our God delights in vindicating even the smallest confidence of His children.

The Challenge

As Christians, we are called, commissioned, and commanded to lay down our lives so that the gospel might be preached to every creature under heaven. Second only to loving God, this is to be our magnificent obsession. There is no nobler task for which we may give our lives than promoting the glory of God in the redemption of men through the preaching of the gospel of Jesus Christ. If the Christian is truly obedient to the Great Commission, he will give his life either to go down into the mine or to hold the rope for those who go down (William Carey). Either way, the same radical commitment is required.

For more information:

Visit our website at **heartcrymissionary.com** for more information about the ministry—our purpose, beliefs, and methodologies—and extensive information about the missionaries we are privileged to serve.